OECD Sovereign Borrowing Outlook 2018

This work is published under the responsibility of the Secretary-General of the OECD. The opinions expressed and arguments employed herein do not necessarily reflect the official views of OECD member countries.

This document, as well as any data and any map included herein, are without prejudice to the status of or sovereignty over any territory, to the delimitation of international frontiers and boundaries and to the name of any territory, city or area.

Please cite this publication as:
OECD (2018), *OECD Sovereign Borrowing Outlook 2018*, OECD Publishing, Paris.
http://dx.doi.org/10.1787/sov_b_outlk-2018-en

ISBN 978-92-64-29259-8 (print)
ISBN 978-92-64-29260-4 (PDF)

Series: OECD Sovereign Borrowing Outlook
ISSN 2306-0468 (print)
ISSN 2306-0476 (online)

The statistical data for Israel are supplied by and under the responsibility of the relevant Israeli authorities. The use of such data by the OECD is without prejudice to the status of the Golan Heights, East Jerusalem and Israeli settlements in the West Bank under the terms of international law.

Photo credits: Cover © Inmagine/Designpics.

Foreword

The 2018 edition of the OECD Sovereign Borrowing Outlook provides data, information and background on sovereign borrowing needs and discusses funding strategies and debt management policies for the OECD area and country groupings, including:

- *Gross borrowing requirements*

- *Net borrowing requirements*

- *Central government marketable debt*

- *Interactions between fiscal policy, public debt management and monetary policy*

- *Funding strategies, procedures and instruments*

- *Overview of contingency funding plans including liquidity buffer practices*

- *Alternative approaches to sovereign borrowing*

- *Liquidity in sovereign bond markets*

Each year, the OECD's Bond Market and Public Debt Management Unit circulates a survey on the borrowing needs of member governments. Responses are incorporated into the OECD Sovereign Borrowing Outlook to provide an update on trends and developments associated with sovereign borrowing requirements, funding strategies, market infrastructure and debt levels from the perspective of public debt managers. The Outlook makes a policy distinction between funding strategy and borrowing requirements. Central government marketable gross borrowing needs, or requirements, are calculated on the basis of budget deficits and redemptions. Funding strategy entails decisions on how borrowing needs are going to be financed using different instruments (e.g. long-term, short-term, nominal, indexed, etc.) and which distribution channels (auctions, tap, syndication, etc.) will be used.

Comments and questions should be addressed to the Bond Markets and Public Debt Management Unit within the Financial Affairs Division of the OECD Directorate for Financial and Enterprise Affairs (e-mail: Publicdebt@oecd.org). Find out more about the Bond Markets and Public Debt Management Unit online at www.oecd.org/finance/public-debt/.

Acknowledgements

The Borrowing Outlook is part of the activities of the OECD Working Party on Public Debt Management, incorporated in the programme of work of the Directorate for Financial and Enterprise Affairs' Bond Markets and Public Debt Management Unit. This Borrowing Outlook was prepared by the OECD Bond Markets and Public Debt Management Unit (Fatos Koc (Head of the Unit) and Gary Mills (Statistician)). Sebastian Schich (Principal Economist) is the co-author of Chapter 2. Serdar Celik (Senior Policy Analyst) and Stephen Lumpkin (Senior Economist) have provided their valuable feedbacks to Chapter 1. The following Steering Committee members (Teppo Koivisto, (Chair; Treasury, Finland); Sir Robert Stheeman (DMO, the United Kingdom); Frederick Pietrangeli (Treasury, the US); Toshiyuki Miyoshi (Ministry of Finance, Japan); Lars Mayland Neilsen (DMO/Central Bank, Denmark); Grahame Johnson (Central Bank, Canada) have provided their comments and suggestions to all chapters of this edition. Edward Smiley (Publications Officer) and Lynn Kirk (Communications Unit) have supported the whole team with invaluable publishing guidance and proof reading expertise.

Table of contents

Tables

Figures

Follow OECD Publications on:

 *http://twitter.com/OECD_Pubs*

 *http://www.facebook.com/OECDPublications*

 *http://www.linkedin.com/groups/OECD-Publications-4645871*

 *http://www.youtube.com/oecdilibrary*

 *http://www.oecd.org/oecddirect/*

This book has...

A service that delivers Excel® files from the printed page!

Look for the *StatLinks* at the bottom of the tables or graphs in this book. To download the matching Excel® spreadsheet, just type the link into your Internet browser, starting with the *http://dx.doi.org* prefix, or click on the link from the e-book edition.

Acronyms and abbreviations

AFT	Agence France Trésor
ASX	Australian Securities Exchange
ATM	Average Term-to-Maturity
BIS	Bank for International Settlements
BoE	Bank of England
BOJ	Bank of Japan
CACs	Collective Action Clauses
CB	Central Bank
CRM2	Client Relationship Model- Phase 2
DB	Defined Benefit
DLT	Distributed Ledger Technologies
DMO	Debt Management Office
ECB	European Central Bank
EIB	European Investment Bank
ESMA	European Securities and Markets Authority
ESRB	European Systemic Risk Board
ETFs	Exchange Traded Funds
EU	European Union
EUR	Euro
FOMC	Federal Open Market Committee
FRDP	Portugal's Public Debt Regularization Fund
FX	Foreign Exchange
GBP	Great Britain Pound
GBR	Gross Borrowing Requirement
GDP	Gross Domestic Product
GFC	Global Financial Crisis
HFT	High-Frequency Trading
ICMA	International Capital Market Association
IFC	International Finance Corporation
IFIs	International Financial Institutions
IFSB	Islamic Financial Services Board
IMF	International Monetary Fund
IT	Information Technology

JGBs	Japanese Government Bonds
LB	Liquidity Buffer
LEA	Liquidity Enhancing Auctions
MiFID	Markets in Financial Instruments Directive
MOF	Ministry of Finance
NBR	Net Borrowing Requirement
OAT	Obligations Assimilables du Trésor
OECD	Organisation for Economic Co-operation and Development
OTC	Over-the-counter
PD	Primary Dealer
PSPP	Public Sector Purchase Programme
QE	Quantitative Easing
SBO	Sovereign Borrowing Outlook
SLF	Securities Lending Facility
SLR	Supplementary Leverage Ratio
SNB	Swiss National Bank
SOMA	System Open Market Account
STRIP	Separate Trading of Registered Interest and Principal of Securities
SWFs	Sovereign Wealth Funds
TEEC	Transition Energétique et Ecologique pour le Climat
TMPG	Treasury Market Practices Group
TRACE	Trade Reporting and Compliance Engine
UK	United Kingdom
ULB	Ultra-Long Bonds
US	United States
USD	United States Dollar
WP	Working Paper
WPDM	Working Party on Debt management

Editorial

The 2018 edition of the Sovereign Borrowing Outlook (SBO) presents some good news, but the legacy of the Global Financial Crisis (GFC) continues to cast a long shadow over public finances.

Central government marketable debt-to-GDP ratio is projected to decline moderately in 2018, but there are wide differences between OECD countries and debt servicing levels remain high. Outstanding central government debt-to-GDP for the OECD as a whole is expected to decline gradually from 74% in 2017 to 73% in 2018, thanks to robust economic growth across the region. However, the pace of debt accumulation has continued in recent years, albeit in a stabilised manner compared to the 2007-2012 period. Changes in debt-to-GDP ratios have differed considerably among OECD countries over the past decade.

The high level of debt servicing, combined with large net borrowing needs, has generated challenging debt service ratios in several OECD countries for the coming years. In gross terms, OECD governments are expected to borrow approximately USD 10.5 trillion from markets in 2018. Accordingly, aggregate central government marketable debt will gradually increase from USD 43.6 trillion in 2017 to USD 45 trillion in 2018.

Looking back over the past decade, the impact of the GFC lifted debt-to-GDP ratios to a new plateau. Outstanding central government debt-to-GDP increased from nearly 50% in 2007 to more than 70% in 2012, and has sat at around 74% since. While some countries, including the Czech Republic, Denmark, Iceland and New Zealand have successfully brought their respective debt-to-GDP ratios down towards pre-crisis levels, debt burdens have continued to rise in some countries, most notably in Australia, Chile, France, Italy, Portugal, Slovenia, Spain and the United States.

Accommodative monetary policy has helped debt sustainability, but may be coming to an end

The long era of low interest rates and a low volatility environment, driven by accommodative monetary policy, has facilitated funding of large government financing requirements and eased debt sustainability concerns in some OECD countries – even though credit ratings of many sovereigns have steadily shifted down since the GFC. The risk-based debt management framework has resulted in relatively well-structured debt portfolios in OECD countries. For example, in 2017, the average term-to-maturity ratio reached 17.6 years in the United Kingdom and exceeded 10 years in Chile, Ireland and Mexico.

Government bond holdings of large central banks reached USD 10 trillion in 2017. This year's SBO suggests a near-term continuation of relatively benign financing conditions, but there are growing concerns that the eventual unwinding of major central banks' balance sheets will bring accommodative monetary conditions to an end. This could lead to a rise in borrowing costs and an adjustment to the investor base of government debt in several jurisdictions. Effective communications by both debt management offices and central banks will remain a critical element to cope with potential challenges in the government securities landscape.

Tools like liquidity buffers can help mitigate funding risks

Sovereign debt management offices aim to fund government budgets at minimum cost over time, and so are regular and predictable market participants. Therefore, funding plans cannot be easily adjusted according to changes in market conditions. On the other hand, several factors, including stressed market conditions, unexpected increases in borrowing needs and temporary mismatches in fiscal cash flows, can increase funding risk which, in turn, complicates management of sovereign financing.

In response, debt management offices have developed contingency funding plans, such as establishing credit line(s) with commercial banks and maintaining a liquidity buffer (i.e. minimum level of cash balance). This year's SBO explores liquidity buffer practices in detail, which countries' experiences suggest is a valuable tool for increasing financial flexibility, as well as enhancing market confidence.

New technologies in finance are driving changes in the way government bond markets function

The widespread adoption of new technologies in finance, such as the proliferation of electronic trading venues, high-frequency trading and robo-advisors, has changed traditional registration, clearing, settlement, payments, reporting and monitoring operations, as well as investment management services. For example, trades can now be executed in microseconds (a millionth of a second). Financial applications using blockchain and its distributed ledger technology have strong potential and, one day, may even enable execution of orders without intermediaries and reduce settlement times.

These developments have substantial implications for primary and secondary government debt markets, and on the wider fixed income market. While these innovative technologies present opportunities, including potentially quicker, safer and cheaper financial transactions delivering significant efficiencies for market participants, they also pose a number of new threats related to cyber-security, algorithm malfunctions and other operational risks. Sovereign debt managers would benefit from diligent observation of new trends to gain a deeper understanding of market developments and mitigating risks, and also to adapt debt management operations to emerging technologies.

Greg Medcraft
Director, OECD Directorate for Financial and Enterprise Affairs

Executive summary

Nearly a decade after the outbreak of the financial crisis, sovereign debt figures remain at historically high levels while elevated debt service ratios pose a significant challenge against a backdrop of continued fiscal expansion in most OECD countries.

Sovereign debt across the OECD area has been rising significantly since the global financial crisis (GFC), albeit at a slower pace in recent years compared to the period 2008-2012. Looking ahead, OECD governments are expected to borrow approximately USD 10.5 trillion from the markets in 2018, similar to 2017. In line with the borrowing figures, central government marketable debt is expected to increase slightly from USD 43.6 trillion in 2017, to around USD 45.0 trillion in 2018. This pattern reflects the continued expansionary stance of fiscal policy in major OECD countries in recent years.

While total borrowing requirements for the OECD area have been stable, sovereign debt burdens remain at elevated levels of over 70%. The 2018 outlook for debt-to-GDP ratio is projected to be 73%, slightly lower than 2017, mainly owing to robust economic growth expectations. The November 2017 edition of the Economic Outlook projects 2.4% economic growth, supported by fiscal policy stimulus, for the OECD area in 2017 and 2018.

Overall, risk-based debt management strategies implemented in most of the OECD area helped governments to achieve relatively well-structured debt portfolios. Nevertheless, the high level of debt redemption profiles observed following the GFC is expected to persist, primarily due to the increasing refinancing burden from maturing debt combined with continued budget deficits in most OECD countries. Total debt service of OECD governments for the next three years is around 40% of the outstanding marketable debt, one fifth of which is due in the next 12 months. That said, high debt service ratios pose significant challenges in terms of re-financing risks for sovereign debt management.

The funding environment has been relatively favourable in major OECD countries, enabling governments to finance borrowing requirements at low cost.

The long era of low interest rates, along with stable market conditions, have created a buoyant funding environment for sovereign issuers in major OECD countries. This, in turn, has enabled governments to finance borrowing requirements at low cost. For example, 10-year bond yields in the United States and Japan, the two largest issuers in the OECD area, were below 2.5% and 0.1% respectively during the past two years, as of December 2017. Furthermore, interest rate-growth differential has been favourable in recent years and has facilitated sustained historically-high debt burdens in most OECD countries. Nevertheless, the current favourable funding conditions may not be a permanent feature of financial markets.

In terms of funding strategies, OECD governments have leaned steadily towards long-term financing instruments in recent years. The share of long-term borrowing in central government marketable debt is estimated to reach around 90% in 2017 and to continue to rise gradually in 2018. Moreover, the average term-to-maturity ratio for the

OECD area rose to about eight years in 2017, and reached unprecedented levels in several countries, including Austria, Belgium, Chile, Japan, Mexico and the United Kingdom. This trend is mainly driven by three factors: Firstly, sovereign debt managers facing significant borrowing requirements aim to lengthen borrowing maturities to mitigate rollover risk. Second, ultra-low interest rates accompanied by low term-premiums which have changed the cost-risk trade-off between short-term and long-term borrowing. Lastly, from an investor perspective, beside the natural investor base consisting of insurance companies and pension funds, a broader spectrum of investors searching for positive yields has created additional demand for long-term bonds in recent years.

Sovereign debt managers take a long-term perspective and carefully consider various parameters including investor demand, additional costs, and impact on existing instruments when making a decision on a new instrument.

The set of sovereign borrowing instruments has expanded over time. Floating-rate and inflation-linked securities have become part of the regular issuance choices of sovereign issuers during the past few decades, in addition to traditional instruments such as zero coupon and fixed-rate bonds. In recent years, alternative approaches to sovereign borrowing, such as green bonds, sukuk, ultra-long bonds and GDP-linked bonds, have been increasingly in the spotlight. This edition of the Outlook describes experiences and views on alternative approaches, following a survey of sovereign debt managers undertaken in 2017.

The well-defined objective of sovereign debt management is to minimise the cost of financing, subject to a prudent level of risk. Accordingly, sovereign debt managers take various cost and risk factors into consideration when issuing a new instrument (e.g. investor demand, additional costs due to novelty and liquidity premium, impact on existing instruments, investor diversification), while striving to support development and maintenance of efficient local bond markets. Against this backdrop, debt management offices (DMOs) of some OECD countries have issued new borrowing instruments, such as green bonds, sukuk and ultra-long bonds, although these instruments were adopted in only a few cases as part of regular issuance programmes. Proposals have also been made by academics and some policy-makers to consider issuing GDP-linked bonds, although no DMO reported having considered issuing such bonds.

Sovereign debt managers have many reasons to desire liquid bond markets and have many ways to support them.

Sovereign debt managers have a vital interest and a great responsibility in continuous, well-functioning government debt markets, since liquidity of government bonds is an important contributing factor in minimising sovereign borrowing costs. In fact, government bond markets have continued to evolve in a number of different ways since the GFC. The combined effects of new regulations, advances in financial technology, as well as macro-economic factors in the post-crisis environment, have reshaped market liquidity in several jurisdictions. Against this backdrop, debt managers take action and implement policies in order to promote efficiency in the government securities market. Sovereign issuers' concerns over secondary market liquidity of government bonds were discussed in previous editions of the Outlook. This edition provides a deeper insight into the key driving forces behind market liquidity conditions in general, and the measures taken by DMOs to enhance liquidity of bonds, in particular.

Chapter 1

Sovereign borrowing outlook
for OECD countries

Chapter 1 examines sovereign borrowing, deficits and debt developments in the OECD area from 2007-2018. It presents current levels and the outlook for gross and net borrowing needs as well as redemption and debt stock profiles. The unprecedented changes in country debt-to-GDP ratios over the past decade are examined and the implications of financing conditions for sovereign debt management, within the context of monetary and fiscal developments and prospects, are discussed.

The chapter also looks at recent trends in sovereign debt credit quality in OECD countries. Deeper insight is provided by a discussion of a measure to quantify and assess credit quality of sovereign bond issuance. The last section provides a brief description of the challenges facing sovereign funding under stressed conditions, as well as the policy tools available including liquidity buffer practices, to mitigate short-term refinancing and liquidity risks.

The statistical data for Israel are supplied by and under the responsibility of the relevant Israeli authorities. The use of such data by the OECD is without prejudice to the status of the Golan Heights, East Jerusalem and Israeli settlements in the West Bank under the terms of international law.

1.1 Introduction

This chapter provides an outlook and overview of sovereign borrowing, deficits and debt in the OECD area for the period 2008-2018. It looks at net and gross borrowing needs of OECD governments in the context of fiscal developments, and considers recent trends in government debt-to-GDP ratios in the current funding environment, as well as implications for funding strategies. Finally, the chapter examines recent changes in sovereign debt credit quality in OECD countries and provides a brief discussion of potential challenges facing sovereign funding under stressed conditions.

Key findings

- In gross terms, OECD governments are expected to borrow approximately USD 10.5 trillion from markets in both 2017 and 2018, to finance budget deficits, as well as debt redemptions. In net terms, the amount of new financing is expected to reach USD 1.7 trillion in 2017 and USD 1.4 trillion in 2018.

- As a percentage of GDP, projections signal a slight decline in gross borrowings from 17.8% in 2017 to 16.9% in 2018, while the fiscal policy stance continues to support and broaden the recent economic recovery in major OECD countries.

- Outstanding central government debt-to-GDP for the OECD area which soared in the wake of the global financial crisis (GFC), has recently been rising moderately. The debt burden, which has remained between 73.5-74.0% of GDP in the OECD area over the past five years, is projected to slightly decline from 73.7% in 2017 to 72.9% in 2018, mainly owing to robust economic growth expectations.

- The elevated level of debt redemption profiles observed in the aftermath of the GFC is expected to persist, primarily due to the increasing refinancing burden from maturing debt combined with continued budget deficits in most OECD countries.

- Market conditions have been favourable over much of the period, generally with low interest rates, and low volatility, which have helped facilitate funding of elevated gross borrowing needs. While downside risks in the short-term are limited, given extended debt maturity profiles and strong growth outlooks, refinancing risks in sovereign debt may pose significant challenges in the long term if market conditions deteriorate.

- The risk-based debt management framework followed by most Debt Management Offices (DMOs) has helped to achieve strategic debt targets and has thus resulted in relatively well-structured debt portfolios in OECD countries over the past decade.

- Credit quality of sovereign bond issuance in the OECD area, notably in G7 countries, has been declining over the past decade due to deteriorated sovereign credit ratings. However, this development has not been reflected in the cost of borrowing.

- In the event of stressed market conditions, DMOs develop contingency funding plans, including maintaining a liquidity buffer, funding from money markets (*e.g.* T-Bills) and drawing on credit line facilities at central banks and commercial banks to mitigate short-term refinancing risk and liquidity risk.

16

1.2 Government borrowing needs and outstanding debt are rising slightly

The 2017 OECD Survey on Central Government Marketable Debt and Borrowing shows stabilisation of government borrowing requirements and outstanding debt figures in recent years, as compared to 2008-2012. Starting with flows, central government marketable government borrowing requirements in the OECD area have increased slightly since 2016, following a decline observed from 2013-2015 (Figure 1.1).[1] OECD governments are projected to borrow approximately USD 10.5 trillion from the markets both in 2017 and 2018. This pattern reflects the stance of fiscal policy, which is set to be eased further to support and broaden economic recovery in major OECD countries.[2] While gross financing requirement figures contain financing needs for annual debt redemptions, as well as for budget deficits, net borrowing requirements represent additional exposures in the market. Net borrowing requirements for the OECD as a whole registered a slight increase in 2017, but are estimated to decrease to USD 1.4 trillion in 2018.

As for outstanding stocks of debt, positive net borrowing requirements reflect the continued growth of central government marketable debt. However, outstanding central government debt, which soared in the wake of the GFC, has recently been rising more moderately. Specifically, nominal central government marketable debt expanded 22% between 2012 and 2017, compared to 44% between 2008 and 2012. It is further expected to rise by just over 3% from USD 43.6 trillion in 2017, to around USD 45.0 trillion in 2018 (Figure 1.1).

Figure 1.1. **Fiscal and borrowing outlook in OECD countries, 2008-2018**

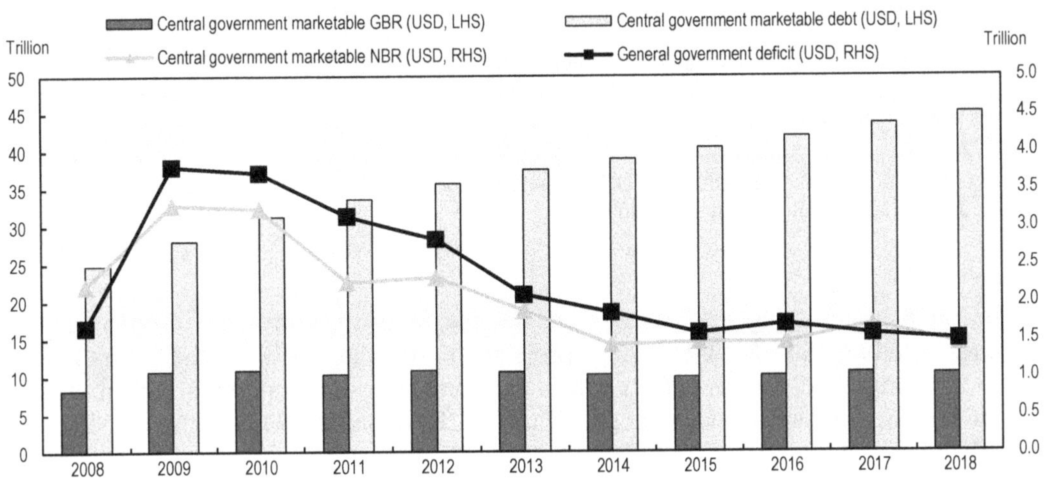

Notes: GBR = gross borrowing requirement, NBR = net borrowing requirement. General government deficit is derived from general government net lending as published in the OECD Economic Outlook No. 102 for all OECD countries, except for Chile, Mexico and Turkey for which the source is the IMF World Economic Outlook (October 2017). Figures are calculated based on data in national currencies using exchange rates as of 1st December 2009.

Source: 2017 Survey on Central Government Marketable Debt and Borrowing carried out by the OECD Working Party on Debt Management; OECD Economic Outlook No. 102; IMF World Economic Outlook (October 2017); Thomson Reuters, national authorities' websites and OECD calculations.

StatLink http://dx.doi.org/10.1787/888933689349

Figure 1.2 illustrates gross borrowing requirements as a percentage of GDP – rather than in absolute amounts – for the OECD area as a whole and for selected OECD groupings. Gross borrowing ratios, which jumped 6 points from 2008-2009 due to significant deterioration of fiscal balances in the wake of the GFC, have been decreasing since then. In 2017 the gross borrowing ratio is expected to remain just under 18%, similar to the previous two years. Amongst selected OECD groupings, "G7" countries' – where ratios are already relatively high – gross borrowing requirements for 2017 slightly surpassed the 2016 level.

Figure 1.2. Central government marketable gross borrowing in OECD countries, 2008-2018

As a percentage of GDP

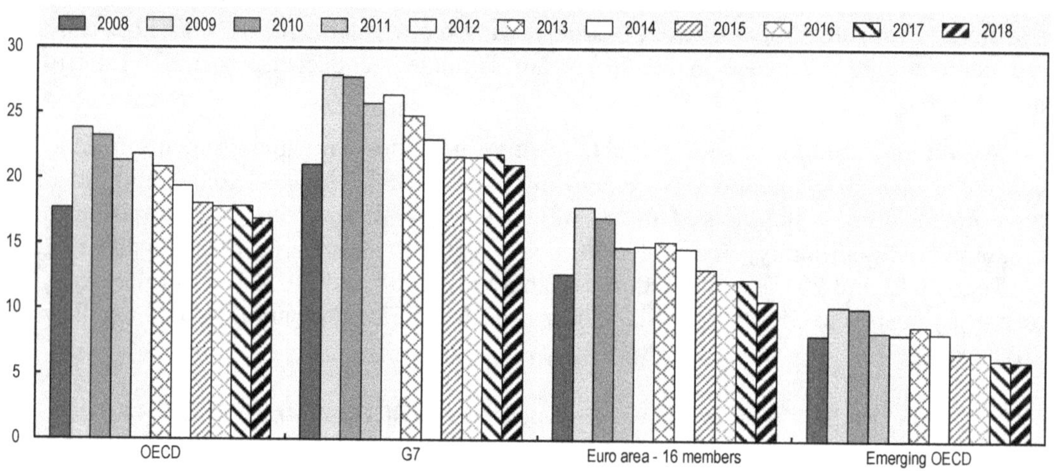

Notes: Central government marketable GBR without cash. Values of marketable GBR and GDP have been aggregated by using fixed exchange rates, as of 1st December 2009, for all years. See Annex 1.A1 for a list of countries in each country group.

Source: 2017 Survey on Central Government Marketable Debt and Borrowing carried out by the OECD Working Party on Debt Management; OECD Economic Outlook No. 102; IMF World Economic Outlook (October 2017); Thomson Reuters, national authorities' websites and author calculations.

StatLink ⟨ᵐˢ⟩ *http://dx.doi.org/10.1787/888933689368*

The 2018 outlook suggests a moderate decline in gross borrowing in all country groupings, totalling 16.9% of GDP and is projected to be more visible in the "Euro area". Overall, the improved figures reflect robust economic growth combined with a stable level of nominal gross borrowing needs. The OECD Economic Outlook (published in November 2017) shows an upward revision in growth expectations for the OECD area to 2.4% for 2017. A similar strong and synchronized economic recovery is projected for 2018, against the background of fiscal easing underway in many OECD countries (OECD, 2017c). In addition to the fiscal easing, the Outlook also highlights the importance of stepping up the pace of implementing structural reforms in labour market and product markets to improve longer-term growth prospects and enhance the overall effectiveness of policies.

1.3 A closer look at the changes in debt-to-GDP ratios reveals significant differences among countries

The GFC took a heavy toll on public finances across the OECD area, pushing debt-to-GDP ratios from 50% in 2007 to 62.2% in 2009 (Figure 1.3). The ensuing European debt crisis further deteriorated gross debt-to-GDP ratios in the OECD to 71.8% in 2012, particularly in G7 and Euro area countries. This means that the average debt burden jumped more than 40% in less than five years in OECD economies (except emerging OECD). Thereafter, the debt burden remained between 73.5-74.0 % of GDP in the OECD area. Despite fiscal consolidation efforts in 2014-16, which helped to considerably reduce net financing needs, fiscal policies in many countries have remained expansionary to support weak economic growth.

The OECD Economic Outlook (November 2017 edition) expects a fiscal easing of around 0.6% of GDP to occur in the median OECD economy over 2017-19, along with strengthened growth prospects. While interest rates on government debt remain less than GDP growth in most OECD countries, this in turn limits a further rise of debt burden (*e.g.* Japan, the United Kingdom). In this regard, the debt-to-GDP ratio for the OECD area is projected to decline slightly from 73.7% in 2017 to 72.9% in 2018.

Figure 1.3. **Central government marketable debt in OECD countries, 2007-2018**

As a percentage of GDP

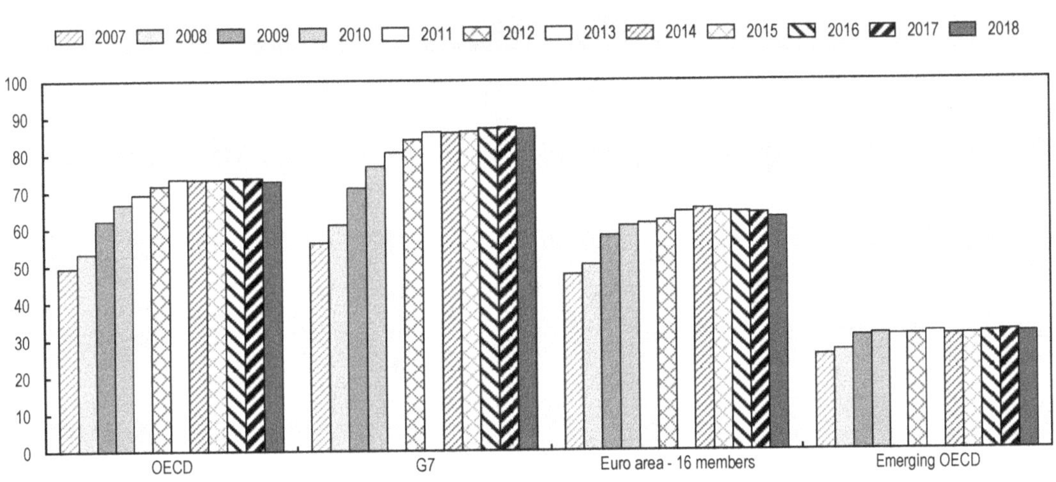

Notes: Central government marketable debt without cash. As of 1 December 2009, values of marketable debt and GDP have been aggregated by using fixed exchange rates for all years. See Annex 1.A1 for a list of countries in each country group.

Source: 2017 Survey on Central Government Marketable Debt and Borrowing carried out by the OECD Working Party on Debt Management; OECD Economic Outlook No. 102; IMF World Economic Outlook (October 2017); Thomson Reuters, national authorities' websites and author calculations.

StatLink http://dx.doi.org/10.1787/888933689387

A closer look at changes in debt-to-GDP ratios reveals significant differences across countries. Figure 1.4 presents changes in debt ratios by country between 2007 and 2012, compared to the period 2012-2017. The results in the first period indicate that public debt burdens deteriorated for the most part in the OECD area, except for a few countries, including Sweden and Switzerland. In contrast, changes in debt-to-GDP ratios in the subsequent span show a more diverse profile. While some countries successfully managed to put their debt trajectory back on a sustainable path, others were still on an expansionary fiscal path. In the former group, the Czech Republic, Denmark, Iceland and New Zealand successfully brought their respective debt-to-GDP ratios down to – or closer to – pre-crisis levels without blocking economic recovery. In contrast, debt burdens have continued to build up further during the past five years in some countries, including: Australia, Chile, France, Italy, Portugal, Slovenia, Spain, and the United States – in some cases even above 100% of GDP.

Figure 1.4. **Debt stock to GDP, percentage point changes over the last 10 years**

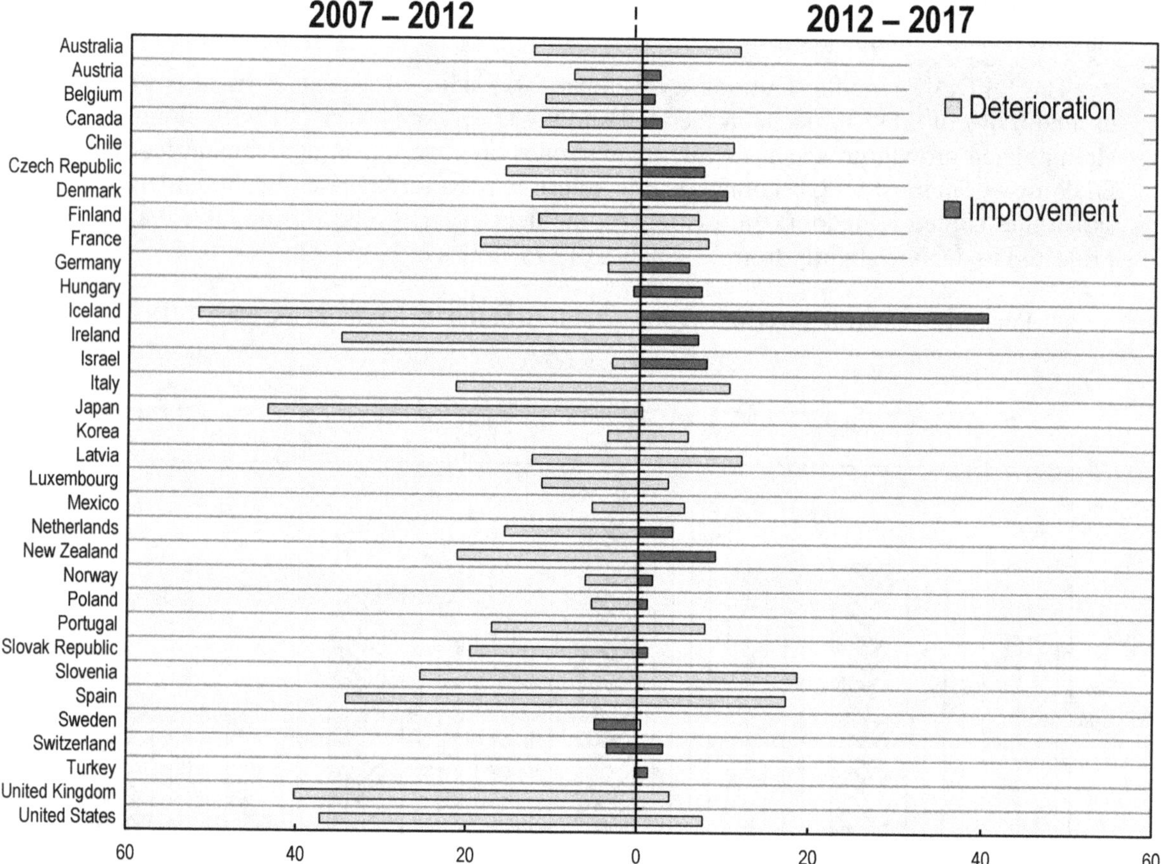

Note: Based on marketable debt stock.

Source: 2017 Survey on Central Government Marketable Debt and Borrowing carried out by the OECD Working Party on Debt Management; OECD Economic Outlook No. 102; IMF World Economic Outlook (October 2017); Thomson Reuters, national authorities' websites and author calculations.

StatLink *http://dx.doi.org/10.1787/888933689406*

The economic growth rate is one of the key determinants of long-term debt sustainability for countries with a high government debt-to-GDP ratio. This puts an even greater emphasis on structural policy efforts (*e.g.* productivity-enhancing reforms) to lessen dependence on expansionary fiscal policies to boost economic growth. The OECD Economic Outlook (November 2017) emphasises that fiscal policy measures need to be undertaken to support potential long-term growth which underpins fiscal sustainability.

1.4 The favourable funding environment may not be permanent

Recently, financial markets have provided a favourable funding environment with exceptionally low interest rates and low volatility globally. This has several important implications for sovereign debt dynamics, particularly in terms of the cost of sovereign funding. Sovereign funding costs in most OECD countries have fallen to very low and even negative levels – up to the 10-year maturity segment – as demonstrated by low term-premia, as well as a downward shift in expected future rates (Figure 1.5). Some sovereign DMOs, including France, Germany and Japan, have issued negative-yielding debt and received premiums from these issues in recent years.[3]

In terms of interest expenses on debt, OECD governments have paid less in recent years, although sovereign debt levels are high, and even on an upward trend in some OECD countries (between 2011-17) (Figure 1.5). However, it should be noted that as the average-term-to-maturity (ATM) of outstanding marketable debt in OECD countries has been reaching eight years, the impact of falling interest rates on government interest expenses has been relatively limited in recent years.

Prolonged low interest rates have facilitated the financing of budget deficits and the re-financing of existing debt in recent years (Figure 1.6.). That said, it also makes economic growth, catalysed largely by expansionary fiscal policies, less costly and more attractive, without complicating fiscal indicators. As such, the decline in interest rates somewhat offsets the impact of the increase in the debt-to-GDP ratio (OECD, 2017c).

Figure 1.5. **Central government marketable debt and long-term debt interest repayments as a percentage of GDP and long-term interest rates, 2008-2017**

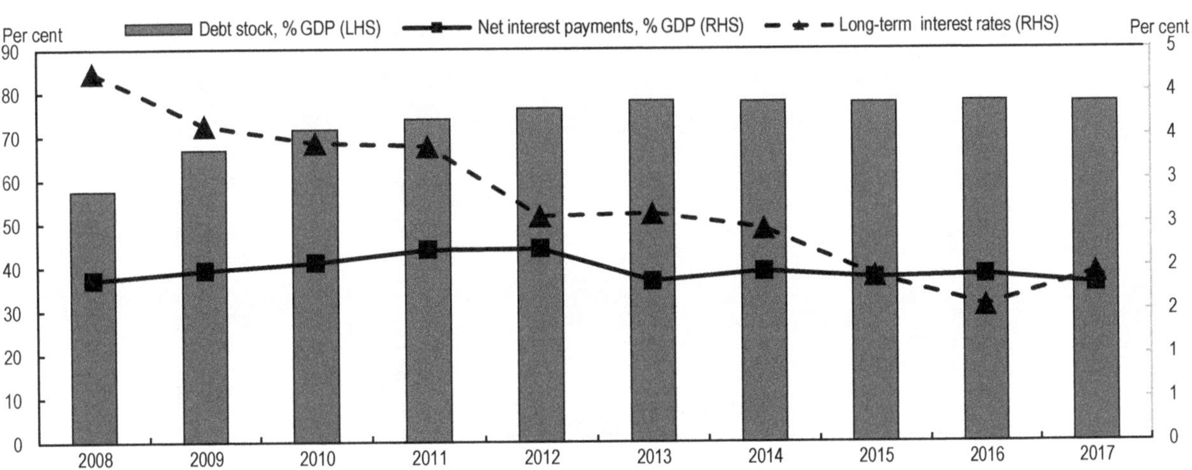

Notes: OECD area estimates. Long-term interest rates derived from long-term interest rate on government bonds calculated as a GDP weighted average.

Source: 2017 Survey on Central Government Marketable Debt and Borrowing carried out by the OECD Working Party on Debt Management; OECD Economic Outlook No. 102; IMF World Economic Outlook (October 2017); Thomson Reuters, national authorities' websites and author calculations.

StatLink 🔗 *http://dx.doi.org/10.1787/888933689444*

Figure 1.6. **Government benchmark interest rates in OECD countries, 2006-2017**

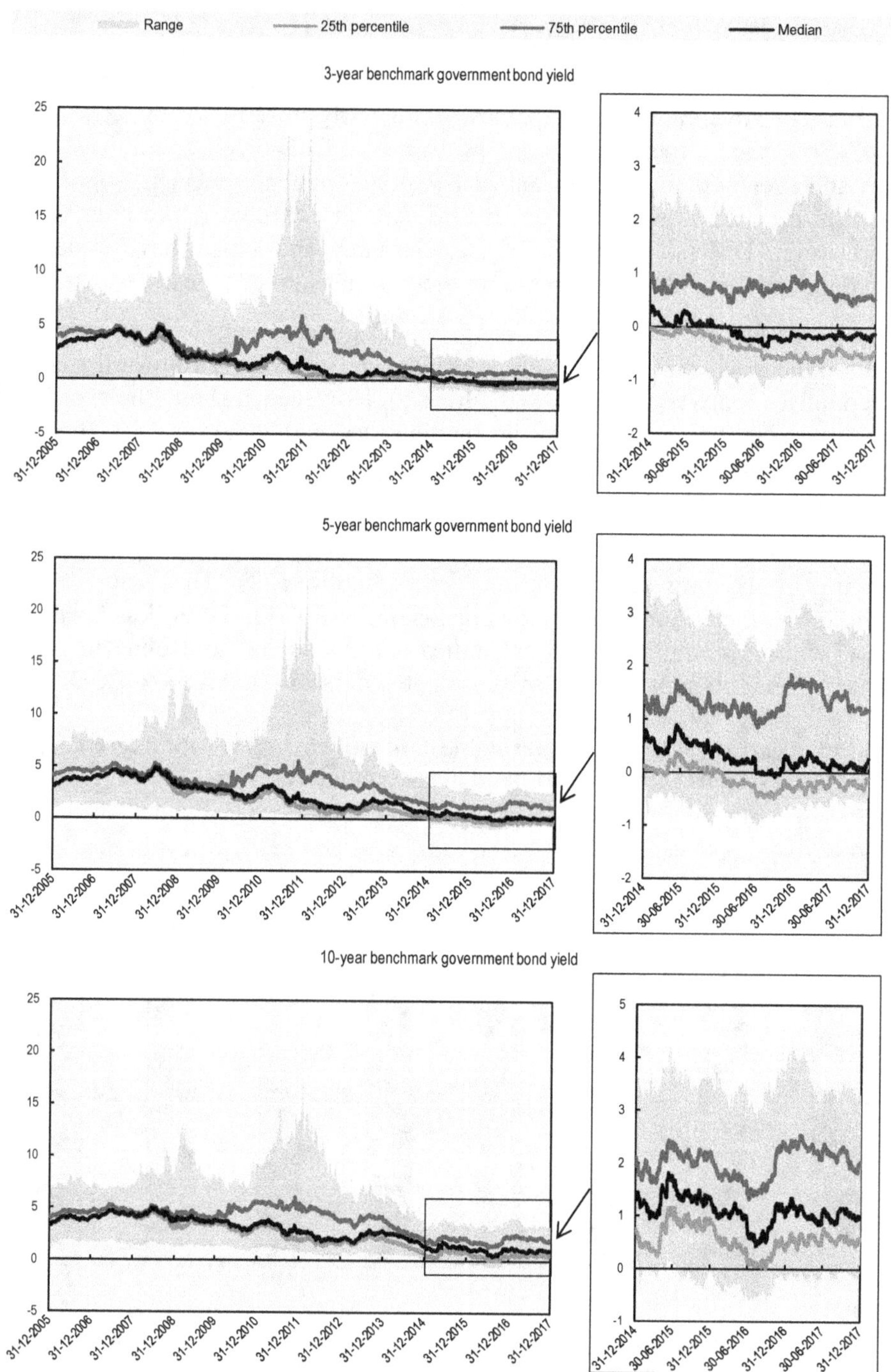

Notes: Interest rates in percentages. Charts show the evolution of several metrics (minimum, maximum, 25th percentile, 75th percentile, median) of 3-year, 5-year and 10-year benchmark government bond yields, calculated for the following group of countries: Australia, Austria, Belgium, Canada, Denmark, Finland, France, Germany, Hungary, Ireland, Italy, Japan, Netherlands, New Zealand (5-year and 10-year yields only), Norway (5-year and 10-year yields only), Poland, Portugal, Spain, Sweden (5-year and 10-year yields only), Switzerland, United Kingdom and the United States. The grey area shows the range of minimum and maximum values among all the included countries.

Source: Thomson Reuters and author calculations.

StatLink ᵐˢ⍧ http://dx.doi.org/10.1787/888933689463

One of the key factors behind the favourable financing conditions is the strong monetary-easing stance that has been maintained by key central banks over the past decade. Specifically, three large central banks, plus the Swiss and Swedish central banks, have engaged in quantitative easing programmes and now hold substantial amounts of government bonds in their portfolios. Today, as large buyers in several government securities markets, these central banks hold more than USD 10 trillion in government debt. As of June 2017, the share of central banks' holdings in marketable government debt reached 40% in Japan and 30% in the United Kingdom, Germany and Sweden (See Chapter 3 for details). These figures indicate the scale of the challenge that debt managers may face in terms of a demand shortfall that will need to be filled during the unwinding process.

Against the backdrop of accommodative monetary policy, set to remain in force in most major economies for the near-term, eventual normalisation of monetary policy measures would lead economic actors to adjust their expectations as central banks become net sellers of government bonds. From a debt management perspective, the drawdown of central banks' sovereign bond portfolio will result in increased funding needs from other investors. Also, depending on central banks' communication policies, this shift might create uncertainty for medium-term borrowing requirements. This process could put upward pressure on sovereign premia and adversely affect market conditions, especially if the unwinding action took place earlier or faster than expected. In fact, leading economists argue that the monetary policy normalisation process needs to be calibrated diligently against the financial market response and the need to support growth along with inflation expectations (OECD 2017c, BIS 2017).

While bond-buying programmes are still being pursued by the Bank of Japan (BoJ), and to a lesser extent by the European Central Bank (ECB), the US Federal Reserve (Fed) had already started raising its policy rate in December 2015 and announced the start of a balance sheet normalisation programme in September 2017.[4] There are a number of potential scenarios that the Fed may pursue but the speed of normalisation and ultimate size of the balance sheet are as yet unclear[5] (See figure 1.7).

Nevertheless, after experiencing dramatic market turbulence following Bernanke's testimony in May 2013, central banks are expected to be more cautious when reacting to monetary policy changes (Bernanke, B.S, 2013). It is important to note that an earlier or faster than expected unwinding of accommodative monetary strategies could shake government securities markets by pushing up longer term interest rates more strongly than desired. Similarly, financial markets often react to delayed or postponed fiscal adjustments, as well as to sudden mood swings, in a non-linear fashion thereby creating the risk of a cliff effect where markets suddenly lose confidence in the government's ability to repay debts (OECD 2014).

In this regard, public finances need to be managed prudently during more favourable times to ensure that there is sufficient room for fiscal manoeuvre when needed, without putting public finances on an unsustainable path. This is particularly relevant given the rise in the stock of debt in recent years, as high levels of outstanding government debt raises the sensitivity of future debt interest costs to changes in interest rates. Generally, macroeconomic policies should aim to strengthen longer term growth potential and reduce vulnerability. This would also create an opportunity for rebuilding fiscal buffers which are critical for governments with high debt burdens.

Figure 1.7. **Projections of the US Federal Reserve balance sheet, 2006-2025**

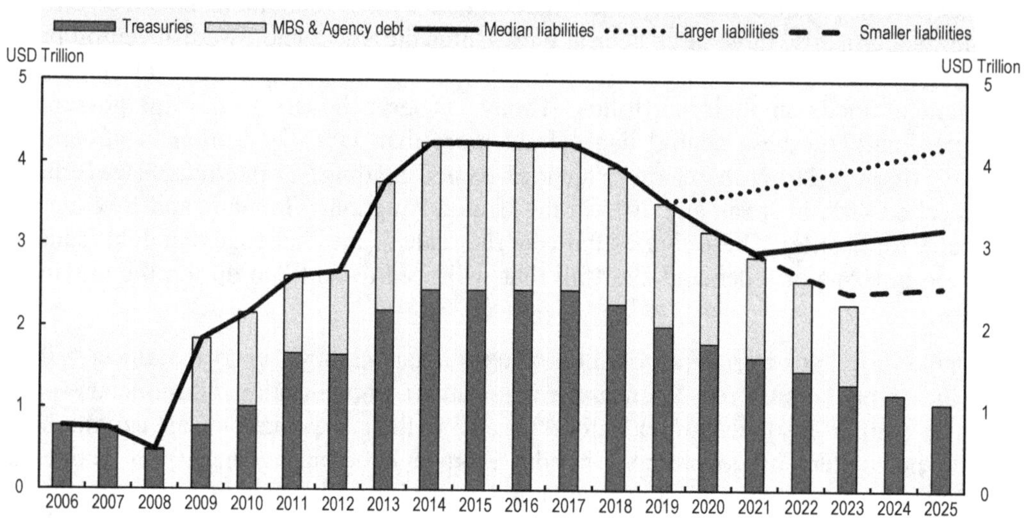

Notes: Figures for 2006-2016 are historical settled holdings. Smaller and larger liabilities projections are based, respectively, on the 25th percentile and 75th percentile responses to a question about the size and composition of the Federal Reserve's long-run balance sheet in the New York Fed's June 2017 Survey of Primary Dealers and Market Participants.

Source: OECD Economic Outlook No. 102.

StatLink *http://dx.doi.org/10.1787/888933689482*

Against this backdrop, and having discussed potential challenges and policy responses during the November 2017 annual meeting of the OECD Working Party on Debt Management, sovereign debt managers are well aware that current favourable funding conditions may not be a permanent feature of financial markets. For example, market participants were surprised by the results of some recent political events, such as the UK Brexit referendum in June 2016, presidential elections in the United States in November 2016 and in France in April 2017 and sovereign debt managers in several jurisdictions were confronted with market swings. Risk premia (spreads) widened during these periods, but returned to normal levels afterwards. In response to periods of political stress, some DMOs adjust their issuance calendar and instrument choices according to market conditions. The impact of political developments on sovereign yields is usually temporary and, overall, debt managers view yields as being more sensitive to monetary policy actions than to political events.

In cases of unexpected market stress (*e.g.* sudden upsurge in funding costs, increasing volatility) due to one or more risks occurring (*e.g.* an earlier or faster-than-expected exit from unconventional monetary policies, delayed or postponed fiscal adjustments), sovereign debt management becomes much more complicated, particularly funding operations, and requires a set of readily available contingency plans. The last section discusses policy tools for debt management, such as investor relations; contingency funding plans, such as liquidity buffers; and medium-term risk-based funding strategies to address funding/refinancing risk.

1.5 Funding strategies to achieve well-structured debt portfolios

The main objective of government debt management is typically defined as "to minimise costs of meeting the government's financing needs, taking risks into account".

When constructing a medium-term funding strategy, debt managers will base it largely on this well-defined objective and take a risk-based approach. This may include the following actions: *i)* identification of cost and risk features (*e.g.* interest rate, refinancing, liquidity and currency risks) of the existing debt portfolio; *ii)* potential medium- and long-term outcomes of a range of alternative funding strategies (*e.g.* constructing an efficient frontier[6] by using scenario analysis or simulation models); *iii)* consideration of expert judgement on market constraints (*e.g.* investor demand, legal restrictions etc.) and potential market challenges and opportunities.

The use of the risk-based framework by DMOs in OECD countries has helped them to achieve strategic debt targets thereby generating relatively well-structured debt portfolios. Table 1.1 displays the evolving composition of gross marketable borrowings in the context of maturity, interest rate and currency choices between 2008 and 2017 and the outlook for 2018. Overall, funding choices have changed in favour of fixed-rate instruments with long-term maturities denominated in local currency. This means that sovereign debt portfolios as a whole have become more resilient to potential market risks.

Emerging market debt managers managing sovereign debt portfolios and executing funding strategies are typically facing greater and more complex risks than their counterparts in more advanced markets primarily due to a lack of deep and liquid local bond markets (OECD, 2005). Currency risk is the most important market risk for emerging economies where local currency bond markets tend to be less developed and foreign currency debt is a significant source of financing. Against this backdrop, the share of foreign currency borrowing has diminished by half over the past decade in the OECD area (Table 1.1), but is still an important part of borrowing strategies in several emerging economies. For example, in 2016 more than 20% of annual sovereign borrowing by Chile, Mexico and Turkey was issued in foreign currency. In recent years, the share of non-residents' holdings in local currency government debt has increased significantly in several countries (*e.g.* over 30% in Latvia, Mexico, and Poland in 2017), implying a higher sensitivity to global market volatilities.

Table 1.1 **Funding strategy based on marketable gross borrowing needs in OECD area, 2008-2018**

(Percentage)

	2008	2009	2010	2011	2012	2013	2014	2015	2016	2017	2018
Short Term (T-bills)	55.5	45.9	44.3	45.0	45.0	43.4	40.4	40.4	41.2	42.9	38.8
Long Term	44.5	54.1	55.7	55.0	55.0	56.6	59.6	59.6	58.8	57.1	61.2
Fixed rate	39.4	49.9	51.3	50.2	50.5	51.1	52.1	52.9	52.0	50.5	54.4
Index linked	2.5	1.8	2.3	2.9	3.2	3.7	4.0	3.7	3.6	3.5	3.5
Variable rate	1.0	1.0	0.9	0.7	0.3	0.9	2.6	2.3	2.4	2.2	2.4
Other	1.0	1.1	1.0	0.9	0.7	0.7	0.6	0.5	0.5	0.5	0.5
Memo item: *Percentage of long-term debt in:*											
Local currency	98.8	98.6	99.2	99.2	99.0	98.9	98.9	98.9	98.7	99.2	99.4
Foreign currency	1.2	1.4	0.8	0.8	1.0	1.1	1.1	1.1	1.3	0.8	0.6

Source: 2017 Survey on Central Government Marketable Debt and Borrowing carried out by the OECD Working Party on Debt Management; Thomson Reuters, national authorities' websites and author calculations.

StatLink http://dx.doi.org/10.1787/888933689425

The rise in shares of fixed-rate, long-term issuance in gross marketable borrowing indicates that the prolonged low-interest rate environment in several OECD countries has enabled debt managers to lengthen average maturity of issues. The trade-off between expected costs and risks of different funding choices has changed due to persistent flattened yield curves in most sovereign bond markets. Looking for ways to mitigate refinancing risks, DMOs of several countries, including Canada, France, Germany, Italy, Japan, Spain and the United States, and have been quite active in issuing securities with maturities of 30 years or more. Furthermore, Austria, Belgium, Ireland and Mexico have sold ultra-long bonds with 100-year maturity.[7] As a result, not only the volume, but also the average maturity of long-term issuance has significantly increased. In turn, this development has lengthened the ATM of outstanding debt and alleviated concerns over refinancing risk, and is discussed in the following section.

In addition to traditional instruments, such as zero coupon and fixed-rate bonds over a range of maturity segments, inflation-linked and variable-rate securities are also part of regular issuance choices in the OECD area and reached 5.7% of long-term borrowing in 2017. Also, some DMOs have issued alternative instruments, such as green bonds (Belgium, France and Poland) and sukuk (Luxembourg, Turkey, and the United Kingdom), but these instruments were adopted only in a few cases as part of regular issuance programmes. Chapter 2 looks at the driving forces behind alternative instruments; key considerations for sovereign issuers (*e.g.* liquidity, investor demand, legal and operational risks) in general; DMOs' experience with green bonds and sukuk and their thoughts on GDP-linked bonds in particular.

1.6 A relatively high level of longer-term debt redemption profile

As discussed in previous sections, gross debt issuance in the OECD area has steadily increased during the past decade, mostly through long-term instruments. As a result of lengthening borrowing maturities, the maturity structure of central government debt, which declined sharply at the height of the GFC in 2008, has improved significantly since then.[8] The share of long-term debt in central government marketable debt reached 90% in 2015 and is projected to rise gradually in 2018 (Figure 1.8).

One of the important implications of lengthened debt maturity profile is the increased ATM ratio which is one of the most common measures of rollover risk. Figure 1.9 displays the trend in ATM of outstanding marketable debt in selected OECD countries. The ATMS is estimated to have reached almost 8 years in 2017, an increase of more than 1.5 years, compared to the pre-crisis period. Among OECD countries, Chile, Ireland and the United Kingdom have the highest ATM.

From a risk management perspective, higher ATM and duration figures imply a lower pass-through impact of interest rate changes on government interest costs and enhanced fiscal resilience. The November 2017 edition of the OECD Economic Outlook suggests that even a lasting increase in 10-year government bond yields of 1 percentage point, compared with current projections, might only worsen budget balances, on average, by between 0.1% and 0.3% of GDP annually in the next three years (OECD, 2017c).

Figure 1.8. Maturity structure of central government marketable debt for the OECD area, 2008-2018

Percentage

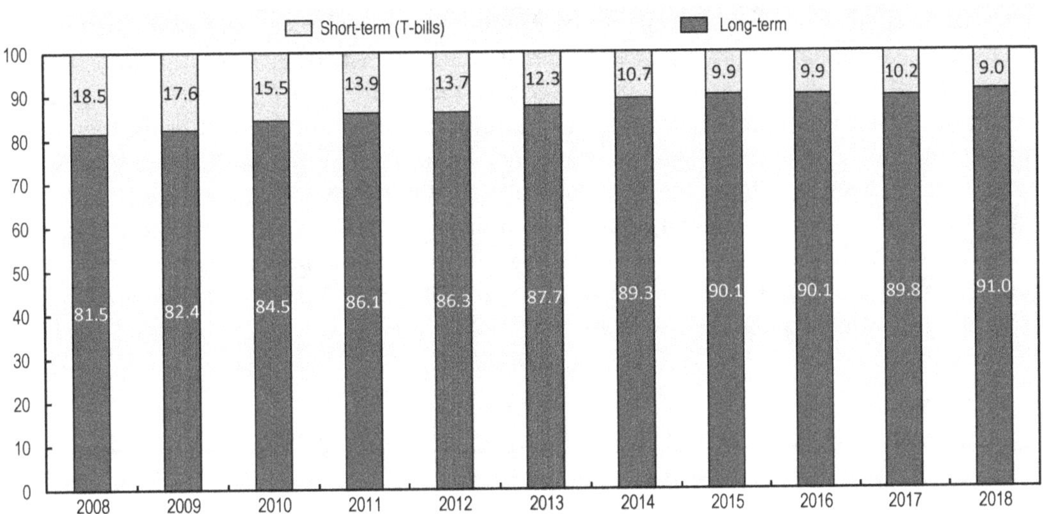

Source: 2017 Survey on Central Government Marketable Debt and Borrowing carried out by the OECD Working Party on Debt Management; Thomson Reuters, national authorities' websites and author calculations.

StatLink ⬛ http://dx.doi.org/10.1787/888933689501

Figure 1.9. Average term-to-maturity of outstanding marketable debt in selected OECD countries

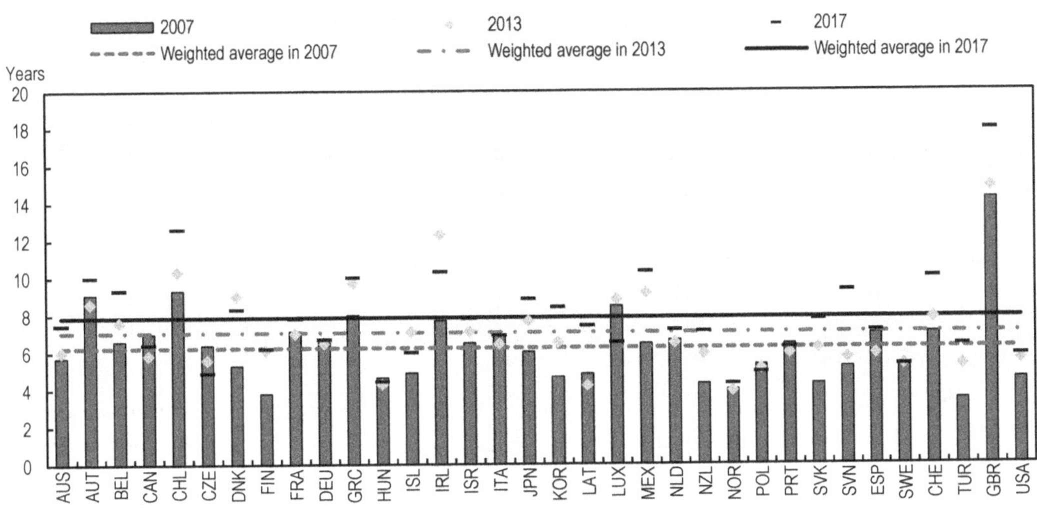

Notes: Data are collected from Debt Management Offices and national authorities' websites. Data are not strictly comparable across countries, see Annex 1.A1 for further details. The weighted average was calculated using data from all countries for which ATM was available for 2007, 2013, and 2015. The values of central government marketable debt (without cash) in 2007, 2013 and 2017, expressed in USD values using December 2009 exchange rates, were used as weights in constructing the average. Figures for 2017 refer to the latest, publicly available, information.

Source: Surveys on central government marketable debt and borrowing carried out by the OECD Working Party on Debt Management; Debt Management Offices and national authorities' websites and author calculations.

StatLink ⬛ http://dx.doi.org/10.1787/888933689520

Nevertheless, a higher ATM level may not always be the ultimate objective for public debt management for two reasons. First, long-term borrowing strategies are associated with higher borrowing costs in a positive yield curve environment (*i.e.* term premia). Therefore, some sovereigns, such as the United States and Germany, with better than average fiscal fundamentals, have stabilised maturities at certain levels in order to take advantage of very low short-term rates. Second, the future path of interest rates remains uncertain, so borrowing costs for a given maturity segment might decline further in the long term. For example, the weighted average maturity of Denmark's government debt soared from 5.1 years in 2007 to 10.5 years in 2008, largely owing to issuance of a 30-year bond with a 4.5% annual coupon rate in November 2008. In the following period of high budget risk, high ATM and duration figures were estimated to contribute to a lower refinancing amount and more stable interest costs for the Danish government's budget (Danmarks Nationalbank, 2015). In hindsight, the high level of ATM limited the pass-through impact of the ensuing decrease in interest rates, on the government's interest expense.

For some countries (*e.g.* Belgium, Mexico and the United Kingdom) ultra-long bond issuance (defined here as maturities of 30 years or more), and discussed in the last edition of the SBO, has contributed significantly to this trend. It should be noted that, in 2016, the size of pension fund investments as a percentage of GDP reached 70.1% in Chile and 95.3% in the United Kingdom (OECD, 2017b). The strong demand for ultra-long bonds is driven by pension funds and insurance companies that are buying long-term government bonds to match their liabilities with long-term assets.

A DMO not only finances net borrowing needs, but also total redemptions. As described in the 2016 edition of the SBO, refinancing redemptions could be considered easier than funding net borrowing requirements, as refinancing redemptions are simply a matter of rolling-over existing debt. However, when redemptions are sizeable, alongside high new borrowing requirements, the DMO may face considerable refinancing risk in the market. In fact, financing elevated budget deficits through long-term debt instruments has generated a heavy redemption profile for the medium and long term in the OECD area. Figure 1.10 shows medium and long-term redemptions of central government marketable debt in OECD country groupings as a percentage of GDP from 2008-2017. Total redemptions of medium and long-term debt in the OECD area have soared since the 2012 sovereign debt crisis, and have remained high, hovering around 8% of GDP. Among the country groups, G7 countries have the highest ratios while emerging countries display an improved redemption profile, owing to fiscal consolidation efforts in recent years.

Looking ahead — unless a strong fiscal consolidation policy is implemented — already elevated debt redemption levels might increase even further and generate additional borrowing needs and gross funding requirements. This clearly indicates a greater refinancing risk in the long term, particularly for issuers with high redemption profiles who may face significant challenges if the current favourable funding conditions are reversed. It is useful to note that in times of market turbulence, sovereigns with weak fundamentals are more vulnerable to spikes in borrowing rates, while "safe havens", such as Germany and the United States, experience the "flight to safety" phenomenon which can translate into lower borrowing costs.

For the OECD area as a whole, governments will need to refinance around 40% of their outstanding marketable debt in the next three years. Interestingly, G7 countries will have the highest long-term refinancing requirements over this period (Figure 1.11).

Figure 1.10. **Medium and long-term redemptions of central government marketable debt in OECD country groupings, 2008-2018**

As a percentage of GDP

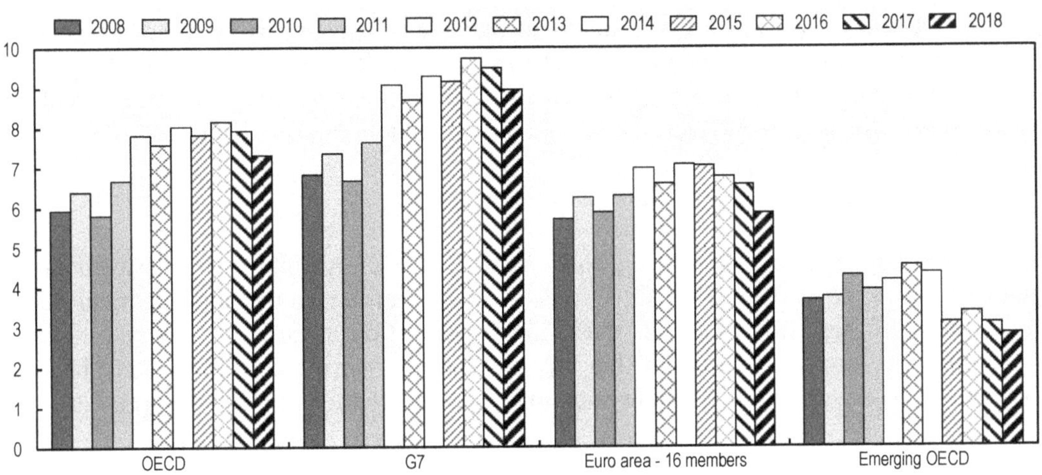

Notes: See Annex 1.A1 for a list of countries in each country group.

Source: 2017 Survey on Central Government Marketable Debt and Borrowing carried out by the OECD Working Party on Debt Management; OECD Economic Outlook No. 102; IMF World Economic Outlook (October 2017); Thomson Reuters, national authorities' websites and OECD calculations.

StatLink http://dx.doi.org/10.1787/888933689539

Figure 1.11. **Cumulative percentage of debt maturing in the next 12, 24 and 36 months**

As a percentage of total marketable debt in 2017

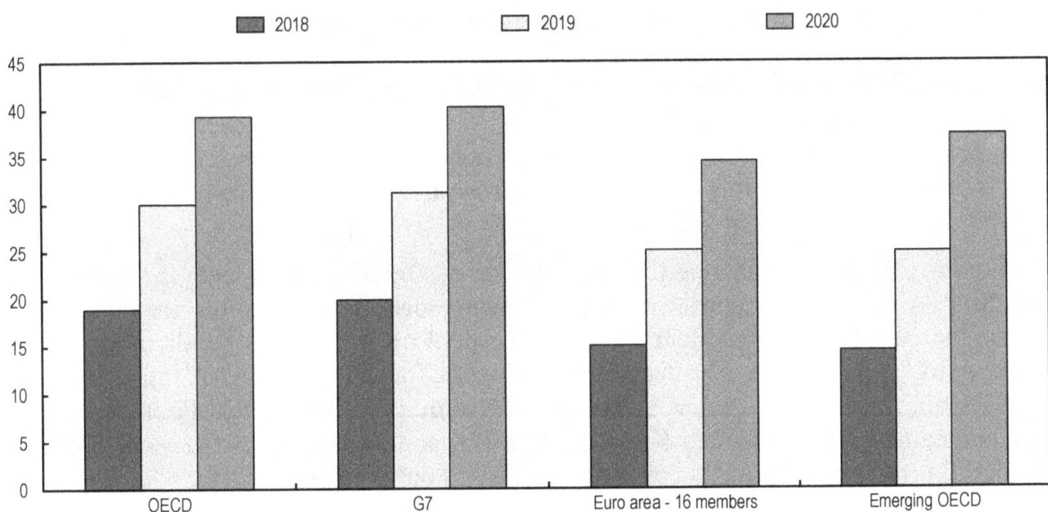

Notes: Cumulative percentage of debt maturing in the next 12, 24 and 36 months (i.e. in 2018, 2019 and 2020), as a percentage of total marketable debt stock (without cash) in 2017. Values of principal payments and marketable debt have been aggregated into a single currency by using fixed exchange rates, as of 1st December 2009, for all years.

Source: 2017 Survey on Central Government Marketable Debt and Borrowing carried out by the OECD Working Party on Debt Management; OECD Economic Outlook No. 102; IMF World Economic Outlook (October 2017); Thomson Reuters, national authorities' websites and OECD calculations.

StatLink http://dx.doi.org/10.1787/888933689558

The high level of observed debt redemption profiles since 2012 is expected to persist, owing to the increasing refinancing burden from maturing debt, combined with continued budget deficits in most OECD countries. As discussed in the previous section, the current favourable financing conditions, together with extended debt maturity profiles and a strong growth outlook, have helped governments to manage refinancing risks in sovereign debt management. However, funding conditions may become less favourable in the long term. To reduce vulnerability to potential market turbulence, it is important for governments to continue their focus on reducing refinancing risks and rebuilding fiscal buffers.

1.7 The recent evolution of sovereign debt credit quality

Theory suggests that borrowing costs should be closely linked to improved credit quality, which depends on fiscal prospects, and macroeconomic and political risks. Assessment of these factors shapes the lender's perception of the borrower's ability and willingness to repay. If and when this link is weak, borrowing conditions may become vulnerable to sudden shifts in investor sentiment and perceptions of sovereign risk.

From an investor's perspective, the main determinants of bond valuation are: the credibility of a government's macroeconomic framework; the integrity of state institutions; the political environment and the country's economic growth prospects. To assess a government's ability to pay, these elements are allegedly captured in sovereign credit ratings.[9] It could be assumed that a government's borrowing costs should largely reflect its credit quality. Nevertheless, besides country specific risks, there are other factors affecting borrowing costs associated with aggregate and contagion risk (*e.g.* changes in monetary policy, global uncertainty and risk aversion) (De Santis Roberto A., 2012).

The perceived credit quality of sovereign bonds is influenced by credit ratings to such an extent that sovereign borrowing pricing largely depends on credit ratings. In general, lower credit ratings are usually associated with higher borrowing costs, in particular during times of market stress. For example, in 2011 during the European sovereign debt crisis, 10-year bond yield spreads between 'AAA' and 'AA' issuers increased about 200 basis points. In today's relatively calm market conditions, the difference is closer to 20 basis points. Considering that governments borrow in large amounts, even small changes in funding rates can result in significant costs or savings to taxpayers.

Figure 1.12 presents the credit rating profile of OECD governments in 2006, 2013 and 2017. A number of countries have been downgraded by the three big credit agencies during the past decade – in effect shrinking the pool of government bonds in the prime category to 11, down from 19 a decade ago. Notably, Ireland lost its AAA rating status in 2009, Spain in 2010, the United States in 2011 (only by Standard and Poor's), Austria and France in 2012, the United Kingdom in 2013, and Finland in 2014. More broadly, credit ratings of many countries have steadily shifted down since the GFC.

Figure 1.12. **Sovereign credit ratings in the OECD area**

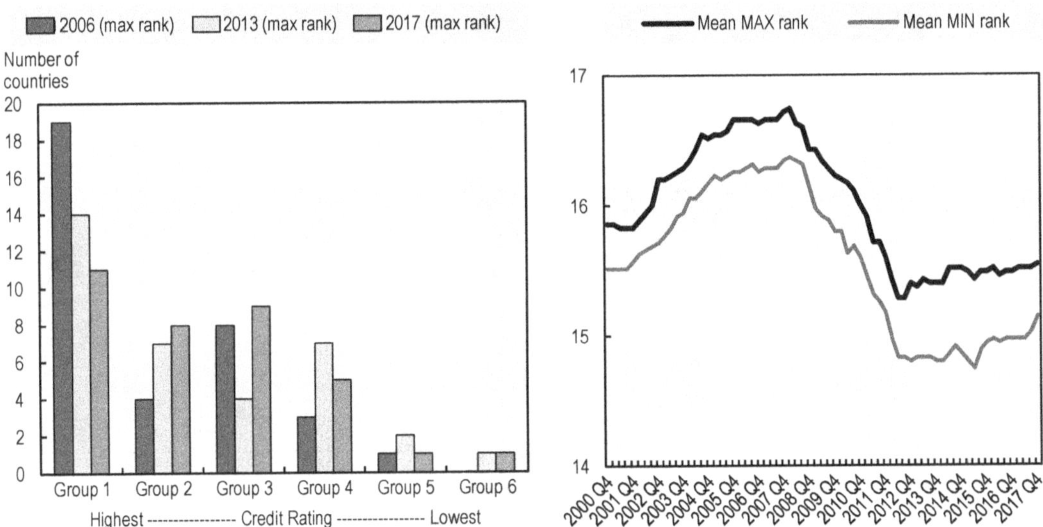

Notes: Group 1 to group 6 corresponds to the highest to lowest credit rating, following these credit rating descriptions respectively; Prime (AAA), High grade (AA), Upper-medium grade (A), Lower-medium grade (BBB), Non-investment grade (speculative) (BB), and Highly speculative (CCC). The max rank is based on the maximum issuance rating from three rating agencies: Fitch, Moody's and Standard and Poor's. Whereas the min rank uses the lowest of the 3 rating agencies.

Source: Thomson Reuters and author calculations. See Annex 1.A1 for methodological details.

StatLink ⟿ http://dx.doi.org/10.1787/888933689577

It has been argued that the size of the pool of high-credit-quality sovereign debt has shrunk, particularly since the GFC. The 2014 edition of the SBO discussed the alleged structural shortages in the aggregate supply of safe public assets (*i.e.* shortage of risk-free assets). It highlighted the definitional and measurement issues around the "safe assets" category, which often refers to AAA-rated assets, and argued that AA and A-rated assets should also be considered as "safe". Using this approach, it claimed that there was no shortage of safe assets, given that the outstanding stock of (longer-term) safe assets (*i.e.* AAA, AA and A-rated government debt) was expected to increase by more than USD 11 trillion between 2007 and 2014, and reach 86.7% of total OECD long-term marketable debt in 2014.

However, caution should be taken when interpreting the results today, given the substantial rise in new issuance of government bonds since the GFC, particularly among issuers rated A and higher, which may have changed outstanding debt quality. To better quantify and assess the credit quality of sovereign bond issuance, an index covering 10-year bond issuance by OECD governments over the period 2008-2017 was constructed. Following the methodology used in the "corporate bond quality index" (OECD, 2017), each issuance is assigned a value ranging from 1 for the lowest credit quality rating and 21 for the highest. This means that a fall in the index indicates declining quality.

The index illustrates evolution of sovereign debt credit quality by selected country groupings over the past decade (Figure 1.13). The results reveal a clear deterioration in sovereign bond credit quality in the OECD area for the designated time period.[10] The trend is clearly driven by the G7 and Euro area country groupings which can be explained by the constant rise in government debt-to-GDP ratios in these countries.

Figure 1.13. Evolution of sovereign debt credit quality, credit ratings weighted by amounts issued, 2008-2017

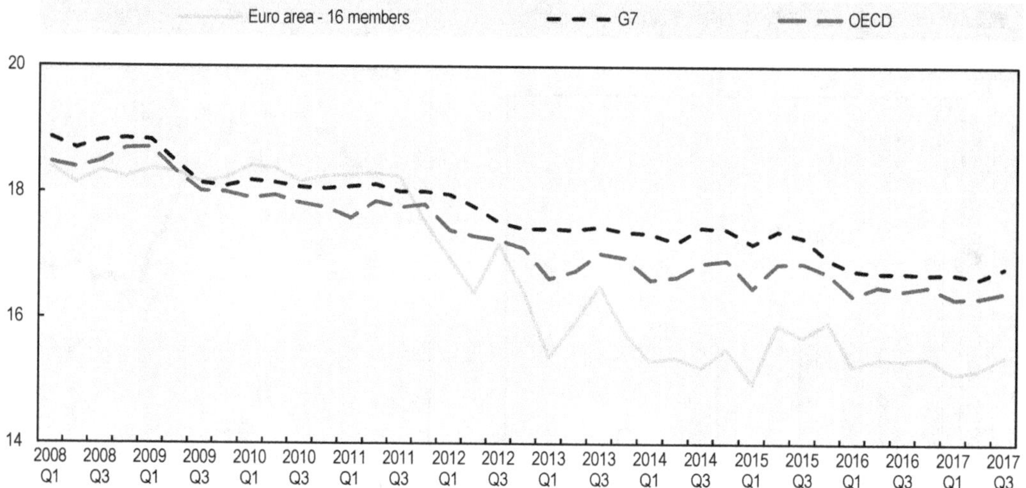

Notes: Weighted average (by amounts issued) and based on the maximum issuance rating from three rating agencies: Fitch, Moody's and Standard and Poor's.

Source: Thomson Reuters and author calculations. See Annex 1.A1 for details.

StatLink http://dx.doi.org/10.1787/888933689596

Furthermore, the distribution of sovereign bond issuance among rating categories indicates two significant shifts during the past decade: the first move was from 'Prime' category to 'High grade' category during the initial years of the GFC, the second was from 'High grade' down to 'Upper medium grade' category (Figure 1.14). Overall, the share of A-rated bonds in total 10-year bond issuance in the OECD area has decreased gradually from above 95% in 2008 to 90% in 2017.

Figure 1.14. Distribution of sovereign bond issuance among rating categories, as a percentage of total, 2008-2017

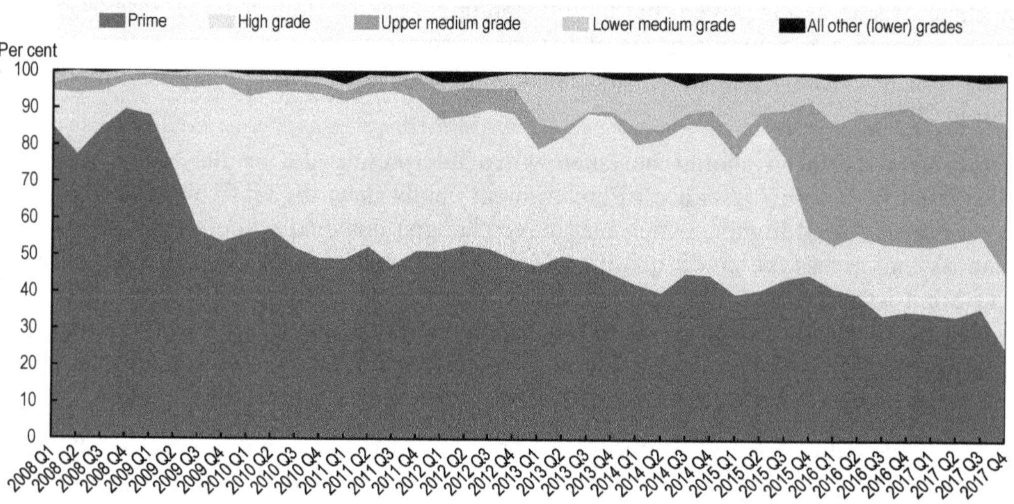

Notes: Weighted by amounts issued and based on the maximum issuance rating from three rating agencies: Fitch, Moody's and Standard and Poor's.

Source: Thomson Reuters and author calculations. See Annex 1.A1 for methodological details.

StatLink http://dx.doi.org/10.1787/888933689615

Given the direct impact of credit ratings on certain institutional investors' portfolios, along with bank capital requirements and pension fund investment restrictions,[11] a downgrade can generate a portfolio shift which can significantly affect bond yields.[12] Although the OECD area has experienced a substantial deterioration in sovereign credit quality, it has had a limited impact on sovereign borrowing costs. Specifically, a downgrade of sovereign credits should have increased yields; however they are at historically low levels in major OECD countries (see also Figure 1.6). This raises the important question as to whether the link between idiosyncratic sovereign credit risk and market bond yields has weakened. These issues clearly deserve further examination.

1.8 Sovereign funding under stressed conditions

Unexpected increases in borrowing needs, short term loss of market access due to operational issues and temporary mismatches in fiscal cash flows pose significant challenges to sovereign funding. Fiscal shocks may occur for various reasons, such as the realisation of explicit and implicit contingent liabilities, a sudden contraction in tax revenues, or military expenses. During the GFC, OECD governments experienced a surge in financing needs and some countries (*e.g.* Greece, Iceland and Ireland) lost access to markets for more than a year.[13] In addition to fiscal shocks, abrupt increases in sovereign borrowing needs can be generated by temporary mismatches between fiscal cash inflows and outflows, overly optimistic budget estimates or market disruptions (*e.g.* a natural disaster). The impact of cash flow mismatches is relatively short-term compared with those of fiscal shocks. That said, sovereign funding can be complicated as the associated liquidity, or funding risk, would be augmented under such stressed conditions regardless of the source.

Against this backdrop, sovereign issuers should be well-prepared for potential future events and should develop contingency funding plans in case of a significant increase in borrowing needs. In stressed conditions, the following actions can be taken, depending on availability of resources: *i)* immediate access to asset portfolio/liquidity buffer; *ii)* issuance of short-term instruments, such as T-Bills and commercial papers; *iii)* increase auction size and tap existing bonds; *iv)* hold large syndications; *v)* overdraft facility arrangements with CBs (*e.g.* Australia and Sweden), and *vi)* credit lines with banks.

Examples from countries with contingency funding plans suggest that maintaining a liquidity buffer (minimum level of cash balance) as a precautionary measure for extraordinary periods, is a valuable tool to mitigate funding risk. In this regard, an increasing number of countries have been setting minimum cash balances in recent years. In particular, the GFC, which put an extreme strain on government financing needs and credit ratings, led more sovereigns to revise their liquidity management policies. The experience of DMOs during the crisis proved the importance of effective liquidity and refinancing risk management to prevent possible threats to the government's reputation and financing capacity. Keeping a liquidity buffer cushions events caused by market stress, which in turn enhances market confidence. A liquidity buffer is considered to increase financial flexibility from both the investors' and issuers' perspectives. In practice, while a liquidity buffer is a useful tool against liquidity strains, idle liquidity balances may be costly due to their opportunity cost. Therefore, setting the target level (*i.e.* strategic benchmark) and investment of the balance are important issues for sovereign debt managers. An overview of liquidity buffer practices in OECD DMOs, in terms of sources, target level, and transparency policy associated with its management, is provided in Box 1.1.

Box 1.1. **Overview of liquidity buffer practices of DMOs in OECD countries**

A liquidity buffer (LB) can be defined as the level of cash, or other highly liquid assets, readily available to cover financing needs and withstand severe liquidity strains for certain durations. Keeping a LB is a widespread practice amongst DMOs in OECD countries with the purpose of managing time differences between cash inflows and outflows, and addressing short term loss of market access due to operational issues (*e.g.* a natural disaster, a cyber attack or terror attack may hinder auctioning debt). A recent survey on LB practices amongst the member of the WPDM revealed that 28 DMOs (including Canada, Denmark, France, Italy, Portugal, Turkey and the United States) maintain a LB as a precautionary measure for extraordinary periods. For example, the US Treasury maintains a cash buffer to provide a cash cushion against a temporary loss of market access due to a cyber attack, a storm or a terror attack.

In terms of risk management, DMOs strive to answer the following questions before addressing a funding risk: i) what is the risk and how likely is it to materialize? ii) what impact would materialisation have on cash needs? and iii) what is the potential cost of the policy response? Various models and methodologies are applied to respond to the questions and set the target amount of the LB. As such, many countries define benchmarks for the level. Since LB is kept in line with cash and debt management objectives, several elements are considered in the diagnostic process to define the target level, including timing, the amount of government revenues and expenses – in particular the debt redemption profile – as well as explicit and implicit contingent liabilities. The most common indicator for deriving levels is the analysis of daily deviations between forecasted and actual cash flows. In general, countries adjust the level in order to cover financing obligations for a certain period of time (*e.g.* survival period) or for a certain percentage. DMOs keep cash buffer levels ranging from 5 days to one year of total outlays, including debt payments. Although levels are variable across countries, the most common buffer level is sufficient to meet one month of debt redemptions.

While a LB is a useful tool against liquidity strains, idle liquidity balances may be costly due to their opportunity cost so authorities aim to manage balances effectively by evaluating all the pros and cons. Cost measures focus on the cost of issuance versus the implied rate of return on LBs. DMOs usually keep LBs in demand deposit and/or time deposit account at national central banks, a risk-free counterparty, and rarely at local private banks. In several countries, central banks do not pay explicit interest (remuneration) but provide a year-end remittance to the government; while some DMOs (including Sweden and Turkey) collect remuneration for their CB account. Country practices suggest investment of excess cash to decrease the opportunity cost. In this regard, the negative interest rate environment in several countries has complicated the management of liquidity buffers in recent years. The DMOs of these countries have reviewed the minimum level of the buffer and put greater focus on active liquidity management (*e.g.* optimising the level of cash holdings with respect to funding needs and/or to current market conditions).

In terms of content, a LB may be in cash, highly liquid assets, credit lines, allocations from International Financial Institutions (IFIs) or other similar forms. The LB can be accumulated in several ways, such as over-borrowing (pre-financing), privatisation revenues, budget surpluses or allocations from IFIs.

Since several entities are involved in different parts of operations, efficient management of LBs suggests an effective coordination mechanism among relevant parties (*e.g.* Central bank, treasury and MoF). Thus, DMOs attach great importance to coordination and communication issues and have developed various mechanisms, such as regular meetings and ad hoc interactions, to improve their effectiveness.

Source: The information provided in this box is mainly based on a survey of LB practices compiled by the Portuguese delegation in 2017, and on general discussions held at the annual meeting of the OECD Working Party on Debt Management on 2-3 November, 2017.

If immediate access to required cash is not available, issuance of short-term instruments, such as T-Bills and commercial paper, increasing auction size and tapping existing bonds and holding large syndications (especially when a flexible and developed money market does not exist) are among the alternative borrowing methods commonly used by DMOs in the event of stressed market conditions. T-Bill funding, in particular, is often considered as a shock-absorber for any unexpected financing needs. Also, this strategy is consistent with the DMO's goal of funding government at the lowest cost over time. While the initial funding choice is the money market, DMOs gradually shift from money markets to capital markets (*i.e.* to longer-term bonds) to reduce rollover risk in the medium- and long term. It should be noted that some countries (Denmark and the Netherlands) that were inactive in the T-Bill market prior to the GFC, had to re-enter the market due to a rapid increase in borrowing needs resulting from the crisis. They faced a re-entry cost which could be described as the re-establishment cost of a bond/bill programme that had been suspended for some time. DMOs therefore attach special importance to being an active issuer in money markets.

When access to market funding is difficult (or only at prohibitively high interest rates), DMOs turn to emergency credit facilities, such as overdraft arrangements with Central Banks (CB) and/or emergency credit lines with commercial banks. The latter is the more common approach in countries where a CB overdraft facility is prohibited by law. Usually, credit lines can readily be tapped at the borrower's discretion after payment of an annual percentage fee; however, this option may not be a reliable source of funding in the event of a sudden downgrade of sovereign credit ratings. In this regard, sovereign DMOs of OECD countries discussed various aspects of contingency funding plans during the 2017 annual meeting of the OECD WPDM. The experience of various countries suggests that, during times of stress, a liquidity buffer is a reliable tool for addressing short-term funding needs and for avoiding a temporary increase in borrowing costs from the market. Additionally, timely and direct communication with market participants is vital to retain access to market funding. For example, DMOs may need to re-activate certain markets, such as T- Bills, at short notice or cancel/modify a pre-announced auction. Noted examples suggest that having an investor relations unit in place in advance of a stress period is quite valuable.

Notes

1. The cut-off date for data collected through the Survey on Central Government Marketable Debt and Borrowing (carried out by the OECD Working Party on Debt Management) was mid-November 2017, and the cut-off date for other data considered in this chapter was December 2017.

2. This assessment is based on estimates of OECD aggregates using the assumption of fixed exchange rates as of 1 December 2009 when converting national values to USD equivalents.

3. Between 2014 and 2016, the volume of negative-yielding fixed-rate bond issues in 14 OECD countries stood at USD 1.25 trillion, total premiums received reached a substantial level, and the maturity of negative-yielding issues went out to 10 years in Germany, Japan, and Switzerland. From an investor's perspective, the demand for negative yielding bonds is mainly driven by expectation of a further decline in yields which would push prices up (OECD, 2017a).

4.   In September 2017, the Fed initiated a plan to gradually scale back reinvestments of maturing securities: Principal payments from maturing securities are planned to be reinvested only if they exceed gradually rising caps – for Treasuries, from USD 6 billion per month to USD 30 billion per month (Federal Reserve Board, 2017, New York Fed, 2017).

5.   As noted in recent statements of the Fed, the future level of balance sheets will reflect "the banking system's demand for reserve balances and the Committee's decisions about how to implement monetary policy most efficiently and effectively in the future" (Federal Reserve Board, 2017, New York Fed, 2017). That said, both the long-run size of the securities portfolio, and the time it will take to reach that size, will depend on numerous variables, including the long-run level of the Fed liabilities.

6.   There is a trade-off between cost and risk considerations. For example, lengthening the maturity of domestic securities entails higher cost but lower refinancing risk. The efficient frontier can be defined as the set of optimal portfolios that offers the lowest expected cost for a given level of risk.

7.   The annual volume of ultra-long bond sales has almost tripled from 2006-2016, as the number of issues doubled in the same period (OECD, 2017a).

8.   Although the long-term trend implies a surge in the share of long-term debt in gross issuance operations, Table 1.1 indicates a slight rise in short-term issues in recent years. As discussed in the 2017 edition of the SBO, the main driver of this development is the US Treasury's strategic policy decision to raise its liquidity buffer by increasing the supply of Treasury bills in May 2015 (US Department of the Treasury, 2015).

9.   Credit ratings are often used as a proxy for credit risk and used by regulators to establish banks' capital requirements. Likewise, institutional investors such as pension funds and insurance companies are obliged by regulations to invest bonds with a certain minimum credit rating.

10.   Unsurprisingly, these results confirm the results of a similar analysis made for corporate bonds, which concludes deterioration in overall corporate bond rating quality (OECD, 2017).

11.   The OECD's annual survey of large pension funds revealed that funds held more than 50% of their portfolio in bills and bonds at the end of 2016 in over half of reporting countries, , especially in Central and Eastern Europe and Latin America (e.g. Chile, Mexico); www.oecd.org/daf/OECD-Business-Finance-Scoreboard-2017.pdf

12.   Empirical evidence suggests that a downgrade – particularly to non-investment grade status – has more significant implications (e.g. currency depreciation and interest rate hikes) for emerging economies (e.g. Brazil in 2016 and Latvia 2009) than for advanced economies (Hanusch, M., et. al. 2016).

13.   Since 2006, Four OECD countries (i.e. Greece, Iceland, Ireland and Portugal) and) have lost access to the longer-term funding market for different periods of times.. Three of these countries (Iceland in June 2011, Ireland in August 2012 and Portugal in January 2013) have regained (partial) market access. However, even when these sovereigns lost access to longer-term markets, they kept (for most of the time at least) partial access to short-term funding markets (e.g. T- Bills) (OECD, SBO 2014).

References

Arslanalp S. and T.Tsuda (2014), "Tracking Global Demand for Emerging Market Sovereign Debt", IMF Working Paper No. 14/39, dataset updated in October 2017; https://www.imf.org/en/Publications/WP/Issues/2016/12/31/Tracking-Global-Demand-for-Emerging-Market-Sovereign-Debt-41399

Bernanke, B.S. (2013), "The Economic Outlook", Testimony by Board of Governors of the Federal Reserve System Chairman Ben S. Bernanke before the Joint Economic Committee, U.S. Congress, Washington, D.C., May 22, 2013; https://www.federalreserve.gov/newsevents/testimony/bernanke20130522a.htm.

Borio C., P. Disyatat, M. Juselius and P. Rungcharoenkitkul (2017), *"Why so low for so long? A long-term view of real interest rates"*, BIS Working Papers No 685, December 2017; https://www.bis.org/publ/work685.htm

Danmarks Nationalbank (2015), "Danish Government Borrowing and Debt" report, Copenhagen, Denmark; https://www.nationalbanken.dk/en/publications/Documents/2016/02/Danish_Government_Borrowing_and_Debt_2015.pdf

De Santis Roberto A., (2012) "The Euro Area Sovereign Debt Crisis: Safe Haven, Credit Rating Agencies and the Spread of the Fever from Greece, Ireland and Portugal" European Central Bank Working Paper Series No: 1419 February 2012, Frankfurt am Main, Germany; https://www.ecb.europa.eu/pub/pdf/scpwps/ecbwp1419.pdf

Domanski, D., H.S. Shin, and V. Sushko (2015), "The hunt for duration: not waving but drowning?", BIS Working Paper No. 519, October; www.bis.org/publ/work519.pdf.

Federal Open Market Committee (2017), "FOMC statement Federal Reserve issues", press release on 1 November, 2017; https://www.federalreserve.gov/newsevents/pressreleases/monetary20171101a.htm

Federal Reserve Bank of New York (2017), "Projections for the SOMA Portfolio and Net Income", July 2017; https://www.newyorkfed.org/medialibrary/media/markets/omo/SOMAPortfolioandIncomeProjections_July2017Update.pdf

Federal Reserve Board (2017), "Addendum to the Policy Normalization Principles and Plans" June 2017; https://www.federalreserve.gov/monetarypolicy/files/FOMC_PolicyNormalization.20170613.pdf

Hannoun, H. (2015), "Ultra-low or negative interest rates: what they mean for financial stability and growth", remarks at the Eurofi High-Level Seminar, Riga, 22 April 2015; www.bis.org/speeches/sp150424.pdf.

Hanusch, M., H. Shakill, A.Yashvir, S. and A.Kranz (2016), "The ghost of a rating downgrade: What happens to borrowing costs when a government loses its investment grade credit rating", MFM Discussion Paper 13, The World Bank Group, June 2016, Washington DC, http://documents.worldbank.org/curated/en/241491467703596379/pdf/106667-NWP-MFM-Discussion-Paper-13-SARB-CreditRating-28-Jun-2016-PUBLIC.pdf

Jackson, H. (2015), "The International Experience with Negative Policy Rates", Bank of Canada, Staff Discussion Paper 2015-13, November; www.bankofcanada.ca/2015/11/staff-discussion-paper-2015-13/.

Koijen, R.S.J., F. Koulischer, B. Nguyen, and M. Yogo (2016), "Quantitative easing in the euro area: The dynamics of risk exposures and the impact on asset prices", Banque de France, Document de Travail No. 601, September.

Mehrotra N. R. (2017), "Debt Sustainability in a low interest rate world", Hutchins Center Working Paper #32, June 2017; https://www.brookings.edu/wp-content/uploads/2017/06/wp32_mehrotra_debtsustainability.pdf

OECD (2005), *Advances in Risk Management of Government Debt*, OECD Publishing, Paris; http://dx.doi.org/10.1787/9789264104433-en.

OECD (2014), *OECD Sovereign Borrowing Outlook 2014*, OECD Publishing, Paris; http://dx.doi.org/10.1787/sov_b_outlk-2014-en.

OECD (2016), *OECD Sovereign Borrowing Outlook 2016*, OECD Publishing, Paris; http://dx.doi.org/10.1787/sov_b_outlk-2016-en.

OECD (2017a), *OECD Sovereign Borrowing Outlook 2017*, OECD Publishing, Paris; http://dx.doi.org/10.1787/sov_b_outlk-2017-en

OECD (2017b), *Business and Finance Outlook Scoreboard*, www.oecd.org/daf/oecd-business-and-finance-scoreboard.htm

OECD (2017c), *OECD Economic Outlook, Volume 2017 Issue 2*, OECD Publishing, Paris; http://dx.doi.org/10.1787/eco_outlook-v2017-2-en

Turner, D. and F. Spinelli (2011), "Explaining the Interest-Rate-Growth Differential Underlying Government Debt Dynamics", *OECD Economics Department Working Papers*, No.919, OECD Publishing, Paris; http://dx.doi.org/10.1787/5kg0k706v2f3-en.

US Department of Treasury joint staff report (2015), "The U.S. Treasury market on October 15, 2014", U.S. Department of the Treasury, Board of Governors of the Federal Reserve System, Federal Reserve Bank of New York, U.S. Securities and Exchange Commission and U.S. Commodity Futures Trading Commission 13 July 2015, Washington DC; https://www.treasury.gov/press-center/press-releases/Documents/Joint_Staff_Report_Treasury_10-15-2015.pdf

ANNEX 1.A1.

Methods and sources

Regional aggregates

- Total OECD area denotes the following 35 countries: Australia, Austria, Belgium, Canada, Chile, Czech Republic, Denmark, Estonia, Finland, France, Germany, Greece, Hungary, Iceland, Ireland, Israel, Italy, Japan, Korea, Latvia, Luxembourg, Mexico, Netherlands, New Zealand, Norway, Poland, Portugal, Slovak Republic, Slovenia, Spain, Sweden, Switzerland, Turkey, the United Kingdom and the United States.

- The G7 includes seven countries: Canada, France, Germany, Italy, Japan, United Kingdom and the United States.

- The OECD euro area includes 16 members: Austria, Belgium, Estonia, Finland, France, Germany, Greece, Ireland, Italy, Latvia, Luxembourg, Netherlands, Portugal, Slovak Republic, Slovenia and Spain.

- In this publication, the Emerging OECD group is defined as including ten countries: Chile, Czech Republic, Estonia, Hungary, Latvia, Mexico, Poland, Slovak Republic, Slovenia and Turkey.

- The euro (€) is the official currency of 19 out of 28 EU member countries. These countries are collectively known as the Eurozone. The Eurozone countries are Austria, Belgium, Cyprus, Estonia, Finland, France, Germany, Greece, Ireland, Italy, Latvia, Lithuania, Luxembourg, Malta, the Netherlands, Portugal, Slovakia, Slovenia, and Spain.

Calculations, definitions and data sources

- Gross borrowing requirements (GBR) as a percentage of GDP are calculated using nominal GDP data from the OECD Economic Outlook No. 102, November 2017.

- To facilitate comparisons with previous versions of the Outlook, figures are converted into US dollars using exchange rates from 1 December 2009, unless indicated otherwise. Where figures are converted into US dollars using flexible exchange rates, the main text refers explicitly to that approach. Source: Thomson Reuters. The effects of using alternative exchange rate assumptions (in particular, fixing the exchange rate versus using flexible exchange rates) are illustrated in Figures 1.3 and 1.4 of Chapter 1 of the *Sovereign Borrowing Outlook, 2016*.

- All figures refer to calendar years unless specified otherwise.

- Aggregate figures for gross borrowing requirements (GBR), net borrowing requirements (NBR), central government marketable debt, redemptions, and debt maturing are compiled from answers to the Borrowing Survey. The OECD Secretariat inserted its own estimates/projections in cases of missing information for 2017 and/or 2018, using publicly available official information on redemptions and central government budget balances.

- The average term-to-maturity data in Figure 1.9 is not strictly comparable across countries. Some countries may exclude some securities (like short-term debt) whilst others may include them. The following notes were received from each country:

Australia	All commonwealth government securities are included.
Czech Republic	State budget debt marketable securities only.
Denmark	Excluding effects from interest and currency swaps.
Finland	Includes marketable public debt securities and thus excludes private placements, loans and retail bonds.
Germany	Excludes swap effects.
Greece	The data refer to long-term marketable debt securities (more than 1 year original maturity) and excludes Treasury Bills.
Hungary	Data excludes retail securities, locally issued FX bonds, loans. Data includes cross-currency swaps.
Japan	MOF announces ATM, based on fiscal year, not calendar year. For the years 2007 & 2013 (excluding saving bonds). For the 2017, the data includes saving bonds.
Latvia	Calculations exclude saving bonds and interest-free bonds.
Mexico	Our calculation of the ATM considers all outstanding market debt (short-term and long-term).
Netherlands	The information is based on the data of T-bills and Bonds.
New Zealand	These calculations include all New Zealand Government Bonds and Inflation Indexed Bonds that are readily tradable in the market. It excludes any Bonds held by the Reserve Bank of New Zealand or the Earthquake Commission. It also includes Treasury Bills.
Norway	The figures represent outstanding central government marketable debt, excluding interest rate swaps.
Poland	Marketable Treasury securities issued on domestic and foreign market, and excludes loans.
Portugal	Excludes T-bills issued in favour of FRDP and used as collateral. Excludes swap transactions.
Slovak Republic	Includes both: bonds and T-bills.
Sweden	Marketable debt securities include: Government bonds, Inflation-linked bonds, Treasury bills, Public bonds in foreign currency, Commercial paper in foreign currency.
Switzerland	Outstanding marketable debt, excludes own tranches not issued yet and securities for cash management purposes, excludes swap effects.
United Kingdom	Treasury bills for cash management purposes, government holdings and undated gilts are excluded from the calculation of the weighted average term to maturity.
United States	ATM is calculated by staff in OECD staff based on all securities data downloadable from www.treasurydirect.gov

Credit ratings analysis methodology

- A dataset of bonds taken from Thomson Reuters (as of November 2017) with the following criteria: i) were still active, ii) having a tenor of ten or more years (or in the case of re-openings – the original issue had a tenor of at least ten years), iii) were issued or had a reopening from 2008 onwards and iv) excluded stripped bonds.

- Credit ratings were sourced from Thomson Reuters long-term foreign credit rating for each of Fitch, Moody's and Standard and Poor's.

- Credit ratings converted into a ranking score, where 19 is equivalent to the highest rating (AAA or Aaa) going down to a score of 1 for CCC- (Caa3 in the case of Moody's), and bonds with ratings below this excluded.

- The analysis is carried out on a bond by bond basis, looking at the minimum and maximum ratings (given by the three credit rating agencies) of the issuer country on the date of issue/re-opening.

- The Thomson Reuters US dollar conversion rate on date of issue (or date of re-opening) was used to calculate issue amounts on a US dollar basis.

- To see sovereign ratings changes over time, an initial artificial dataset was created which gave every country exactly one issue in each quarter. Based on this artificial dataset, a table was constructed to count the number of bonds (*i.e.* countries) with each credit rating rank in each quarter, of which the mean ranking was then calculated for each quarter.

- For the analysis which is weighted by amount: A table was constructed to sum the total amount issued in US Dollars in each quarter within each credit rating rank of which the weighted mean for the ranking was then calculated for each quarter (see figure 1.13 for the presentation of this analysis).

Chapter 2

Alternative approaches to sovereign borrowing

The set of instruments issued by sovereign debt managers has expanded over time. Floating-rate and inflation-linked securities have become part of regular issuance choices over the past few decades in addition to traditional instruments, such as zero coupon and fixed rate bonds over a range of maturity segments. In recent years, alternative approaches to sovereign borrowing, such as green bonds and sukuk, have been increasingly in the spotlight. Debt management offices of some OECD countries have issued these instruments mainly to attract investors with different mandates. Nevertheless, only a few countries adopted them as part of regular issuance programmes. Counter-cyclical instruments, including GDP-linked bonds, have also been widely discussed at a theoretical level and in particular their potential role in providing a countercyclical cushion for governments.

This chapter draws on discussions and work undertaken by the Committee on Financial Markets and the Working Party on Debt Management, and focuses on: the main drivers for alternative approaches; key considerations for sovereign issuers; issuers' experience with green bonds and sukuk; as well as views on new approaches, including GDP-linked bonds. In addition, the growing issuance of ultra-long bonds is elaborated in terms of the driving forces and potential implications for investors and issuers.

The statistical data for Israel are supplied by and under the responsibility of the relevant Israeli authorities. The use of such data by the OECD is without prejudice to the status of the Golan Heights, East Jerusalem and Israeli settlements in the West Bank under the terms of international law.

2.1 Introduction

Sovereign issuers have a long history of financial innovation in designing sovereign funding products. They launch new financial products, or modify the structure of existing products, in order to attract investors and adapt to their needs. In this chapter, the benefits and challenges of introducing new products to sovereign debt markets are discussed with a special focus on recent examples.

Key findings

- Sovereign debt managers take a long-term perspective and consider various parameters (e.g. investor demand, additional costs due to novelty and liquidity premium, impact on existing instruments, investor diversification), when making a decision on a new instrument. They monitor primary and secondary market developments closely, and assess changing investor needs to help devise an appropriate strategy with suitable instruments for financing budget deficits.

- Issuers of alternative borrowing instruments which may encompass pricing complications prefer to employ syndication and private placement methods for inaugural issuance (e.g. sukuk issuance by Luxembourg, Turkey and the United Kingdom, green bond issuance by Belgium, France and Poland) as an attempt to mitigate potential difficulties that investors face during the price discovery process.

- Proposals have been made by academics and some policy-makers to consider issuing GDP-linked bonds, although no debt management office (DMO) reported having considered issuance of such bonds feasible. Novelty, liquidity and indexation premium of such debt may be high. Experience with the issuance of inflation-linked bonds suggests that while the liquidity premium tended initially to be higher than for comparable conventional nominal debt, it declined over time as the new inflation-linked programme gained maturity.

- From a sovereign debt managers' perspective, the existence of market demand is less of an issue for green bonds, and to some extent for sukuk bonds, as institutional investors committed to these distinctive market segments are already present. However, high administrative requirements (e.g. monitoring and reporting activities), special marketing activities and legislative changes are considered as major challenges to issuance of green bonds.

- Experiences with sukuk issuance in a few OECD countries suggest that the main impediments to issuing this instrument are the high legal costs to structure the product in accordance with Islamic finance requirements, as well as the associated multifaceted transactions.

- Ultra-long government bond issuance has been increasing in recent years with the intention of reducing refinancing risk, as well as taking advantage of a low yield environment. Yet, concerns over the presence of strong and sustainable investor demand for such debt and the potential adverse impact on existing long-term bonds restrain some potential issuers.

2.2 Main drivers for alternative approaches

It is notoriously difficult to define "standard" or "alternative" sovereign debt instruments, as the notion of "standard" differs across countries and changes over time. For example, issuance of sovereign bonds with principal and/or coupon linked to the level of a state variable, such as inflation, was uncommon among OECD economies during the 1980s. By the beginning of 2000 however they were considered a well-established class of sovereign bonds by some sovereign debt issuers (Thedéen, 2004). Currently such bonds are issued by many sovereigns and could thus be considered "standard". The potential issuance of yet another type of state-contingent bond i.e. bonds with payments linked to GDP indices, was discussed recently by policy makers at the 2017 meetings of the OECD's Committee on Financial Markets in April and the Working Party on Debt Management in November.

The use of sovereign debt instruments has expanded as policy makers respond to changes in the macroeconomic environment, financial market landscapes, and investors' needs. In addition to traditional instruments such as zero coupon and fixed rate bonds, floating-rate and inflation-linked securities have become part of regular issuance choices in many countries during the past few decades. More recently, 'alternative approaches' to sovereign borrowing, including green bonds and sukuk, have been increasingly in the spotlight.

For the purpose of this chapter, an instrument is considered as an 'alternative approach', if it is not a common practice (i.e. not commonly used in sovereign financing programmes) in the OECD area and requires one or more of the following activities: i) changes in the existing legislative framework; ii) additional administrative requirements, such as designing a new instrument, changing/creating monitoring and reporting systems; iii) special marketing activities. In the light of recent developments, special focus is given to experience with green bonds, sukuks, ultra-long bonds and views on GDP-linked instruments.

Historically, the evolution of financial markets has been driven by the need to mitigate various challenges, and innovations in financial instruments are no exception to this. For example, one of the most critical aspects of fund management is protection against a loss of purchasing power. When the price level in an economy is volatile and expected to increase in the future, the situation increases risk for the real value of asset portfolios. Therefore, investors seek hedging instruments to protect their savings from the negative impact of inflation and potentially increase their future purchasing power. In this respect, inflation-linked instruments provide almost perfect hedges against losses due to rising price levels.

The introduction of inflation-linked bonds and floating rate notes in sovereign debt markets differs widely in the OECD area. Inflation-linked sovereign bonds were integrated into sovereign financing programmes in 21 OECD countries at various times since the 1980s (e.g. the United Kingdom in 1981, Australia in 1985, Canada in 1991, Sweden in 1994, the United States in 1997, France in 1998, Italy and Japan in 2003, and Germany in 2006).

2.3 Key debt management considerations when issuing a new instrument

The sovereign debt managers' mandate can be described as "to minimise the cost of financing, subject to a prudent level of risk". In line with their core mandate, sovereign debt managers take into consideration various cost and risk factors associated with issuing a new instrument while striving to support development and maintenance of efficient local bond markets. DMOs attach great importance to the potential adverse impacts of issuing a new instrument on the liquidity of existing instruments, as well as the associated additional costs of issuance. It should be noted that entering a new market requires a long-term commitment to create and maintain liquidity and to lower issuance cost. Against this backdrop, sovereign issuers monitor primary and secondary market developments closely, and assess changing investor needs to help devise an appropriate strategy for raising the necessary financing for government.

A 2017 survey of OECD Working Party on Debt Management (WPDM) members on alternative approaches to sovereign borrowing reveals important policy information. Survey results show that, when an alternative borrowing instrument is introduced, sovereign issuers consider a list of parameters: i) potential impact on existing instruments; ii) additional costs due to novelty and liquidity premia; iii) strength and sustainability of investor demand across interest rate cycles; iv) expanding investor base; v) complications around pricing of a new instrument; vi) portfolio diversification and risk reduction; vii) governmental decisions; viii) playing a leading role in developing a market segment (Figure 2.1).

Figure 2.1. **Key factors in the decision to issue an alternative instrument**

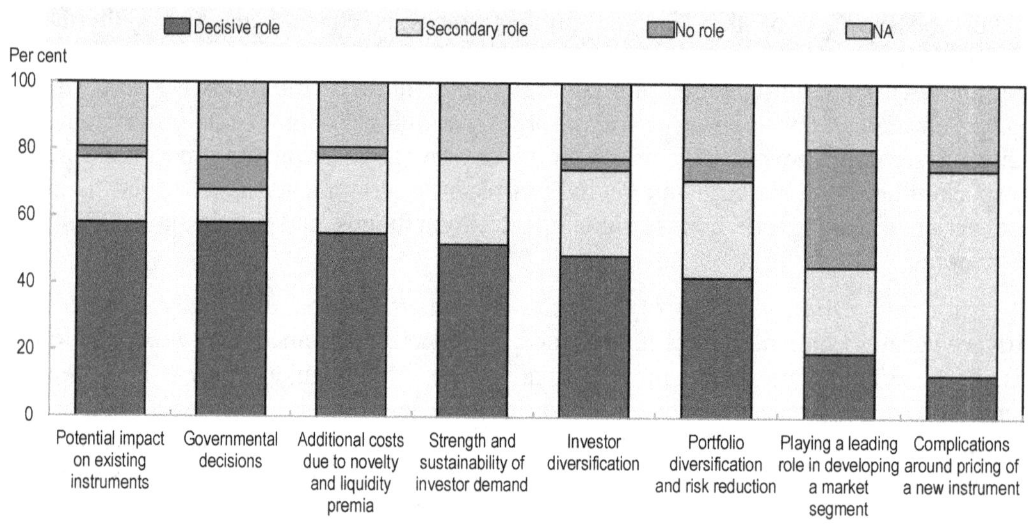

Source: 2017 Survey on Alternative Approaches to Sovereign Borrowing carried out by the OECD Working Party on Debt Management.

StatLink http://dx.doi.org/10.1787/888933689634

During its 2017 annual meeting, OECD WPDM members elaborated on key considerations to be taken into account when issuing a new borrowing instrument based on the survey results. Sovereign debt managers highlighted that the prerequisite for launching a new instrument is consistency with the debt management objective and principles on which the debt management policy is based. In this regard, potential opportunities and obstacles associated with issuing a new instrument are evaluated diligently in the context of a variety of cost (e.g. liquidity and novelty premium) and risk (e.g. legal and operational risk) factors.

It is important to note that some countries, especially those with decreasing or small funding needs (e.g. Denmark, Finland, the Netherlands and Sweden), refrain from introducing new instruments to avoid potential 'crowding out' of existing traditional bonds. When a large group of investors shift from an existing maturity segment to a new one, this development can undermine market liquidity for the existing segment. Even for sizable markets, the potential "cannibalisation" of liquidity in existing bonds with similar maturities is a source of concern.

Nevertheless, observing increasing investor demand for a new instrument encourages potential issuers, especially when budget deficits are substantial. For example, some countries noted they may consider issuing green bonds as the number of investors, such as large Sovereign Wealth Funds (SWFs) and pension funds, that are committed to responsible investment and integration of environmental, social and governance factors into their investment processes has increased in recent years.

In terms of the decision-making process, DMOs in many countries rely on an expert panel/committee to assess relevance of a new instruments according to the factors listed above. Some DMOs (e.g. Austria, Finland, France, Germany and Turkey) have specific formal guidelines (e.g. a set of principles) that the new instruments must comply with. Preliminary cost and benefit analysis of a new instrument is carried out according to internal guidelines which enables decision makers to comprehensively assess the new instrument. Operational aspects and technical features of the instrument are generally designed once the policy decision has been made.

Figure 2.2 **DMOs on green bonds, sukuk and GDP-linked instruments**

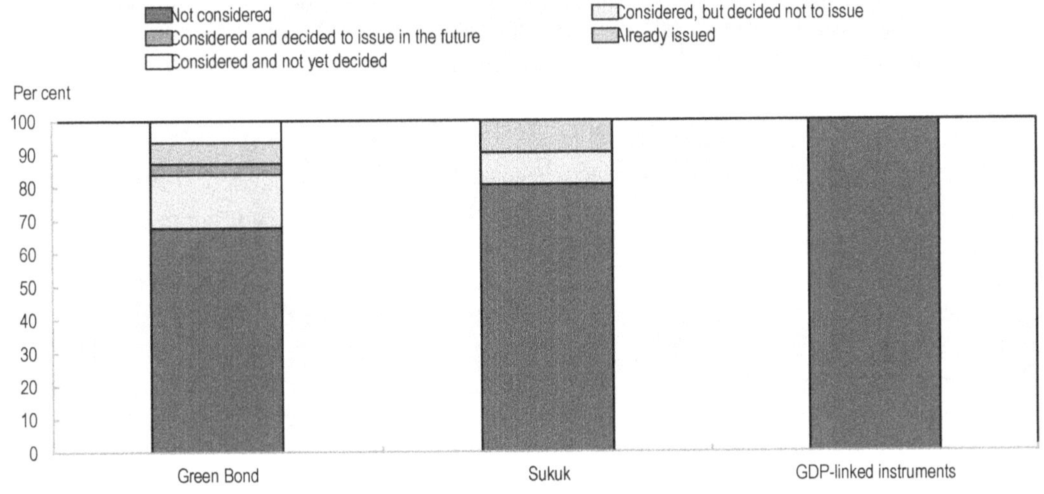

Source: 2017 Survey on Alternative Approaches to Sovereign Borrowing carried out by the OECD Working Party on Debt Management.

StatLink http://dx.doi.org/10.1787/888933689653

The survey also asked if DMOs have considered green bond, sukuk or GDP-linked instruments in recent years, and the outcome of the decision. In the OECD area, two countries launched green bonds (France and Poland) and three countries launched sukuk (Luxembourg, Turkey and the United Kingdom). Survey results show that the green bond, in relative terms, is the most popular alternative instrument, while GDP-linked instruments have not yet been considered by any DMO (Figure 2.2).

2.4 The evolving market for new sovereign debt instruments: Lessons learned from experiences with inflation-indexed bonds

Global volumes of inflation-index-linked government bonds increased significantly over the last decade, with sovereigns from France, the United Kingdom, and the United States among the largest issuers of these securities. Inflation-index-linked bonds, sometimes simply referred to as "linkers", offer a nearly perfect direct hedge against inflation, and institutional investors with liabilities that increase with inflation are natural investors[1] in such securities. Inflation-linked debentures are not particularly new. In the United States, as early as 1742, Massachusetts (then known as the Massachusetts Bay Colony) issued money market securities that were linked to the price of silver on the London Stock Exchange. More recently, inflation-linked bonds were issued by governments in Finland in 1945 and Israel in 1955. Such securities became more widely spread after the UK government issued them in 1981. Australia followed in 1985, Canada in 1991, Sweden in 1994, the United States in 1997, France in 1998, Italy in 2003, Japan in 2004, and Germany in 2006. Today, the majority of OECD countries are issuing inflation-linked sovereign bonds.

Notably, all the first issuances of sovereign inflation-linked securities occurred in varied inflation environments. For example, domestic inflation was high when Israel and the United Kingdom introduced linkers and was low when Germany and Japan introduced them.

While inflation protection concerns play a role in investor demand for such securities, specific motivations vary across countries and time. In fact, despite specific advantages that have been identified, in theory, as potentially supporting demand for inflation-linked securities, the strength of actual investor interest in these bonds has sometimes been difficult to explain (Théden, 2004). In Sweden, Debt Office managed very substantial cost savings, given that the market priced in an inflation rate which turned out to be consistently lower than market expectations.

Looking across the OECD area, while issuance of inflation-indexed government debt was fairly limited during the 1980s, it became gradually more common and important during subsequent decades (OECD, 2017). Nominal payments of inflation-indexed bonds grow with inflation, so that real returns for buy-and-hold investors are fixed at the bonds purchase time regardless of subsequent inflation developments. The purchaser is thus protected against inflation increases, especially those that exceed expectations at the time of purchase. Buying protection against the uncertainties of the future inflation path is motivation for investors to purchase inflation-indexed-linked debt. Bonds offering such protection are of particular interest to pension funds and insurance companies, whose future obligations are linked to nominal developments because of indexation of pensions or policyholder benefits. Investing in inflation-linked bonds offers these financial intermediaries the opportunity to more closely match assets with liabilities, in the sense that the risk of deviation, as a result of inflation, between the two sides of the balance sheet is reduced. For example, Danmarks Nationalbank Government Debt Management explain that the introduction of inflation linkers in May 2012 met with a rising structural demand for inflation-linked bonds, given the transition in part towards pension schemes without nominal guarantees, and to the pension sector's growing focus on ensuring long-term purchasing power of pensions rather than achieving specific nominal returns.

That said, the relative importance of inflation-linkers as part of a sovereign's total debt has increased in an environment of low inflation. And despite the reduction of observed break-even inflation rates[2] over recent years, issuance of inflation-linked bonds did not falter due to the demand from pension funds and insurance companies which remained strong, even in the current low inflation environment. In fact, in some countries the share of inflation-indexed government debt as part of total outstanding government debt has increased over time and exceeds double-digit percentages. For example, in the United Kingdom, the share is high at over 25% as of 2017. However, the share has remained much lower, elsewhere. Also, issuance of inflation-indexed bonds has been suspended or discontinued in some countries. Table 2.1 provides some summary statistics of inflation-linker programmes in selected OECD countries.

Table 2.1. **Inflation-linked issuance programmes in selected OECD countries**

Country	Date when started	Current status/ Date when suspended
Australia	1985	No new issue since 2003
Canada	1994	Ongoing
Denmark	2012	Ongoing
France	1998	Ongoing
Germany	2006	Ongoing
Italy	2003	Ongoing
New Zealand	1996	Suspended in 1999
Sweden	1994	Ongoing
United Kingdom	1981	Ongoing
United States	1997	Ongoing

Source: Update and extension from Shen (2009).

Figure 2.3 describes how issuance of index-linked bonds has evolved in the OECD area, based on data collected through the Survey on Central Government Marketable Debt and Borrowing undertaken by the OECD Working Party on Debt Management (and including OECD staff projections for 2018). Since 2011, the stock of inflation linkers has grown annually in both nominal terms and as a percentage of central government debt. In 2017, the annual growth in nominal terms exceeded 5% whilst the share of linkers as a percentage of central debt grew by over 1%. Both the volume of linkers and their percentage share of central government debt is expected to increase further in 2018 and to reach around USD 3.5 trillion or 7.8% of central government debt. These aggregates hide considerable differences across countries. Outstanding volumes of index-linked bonds as a share of total domestic sovereign debt outstanding are considerable in Chile and Israel, while the total volume of inflation-linked debt is particularly high in the case of the United States. Other major markets for linkers include France, Italy and the United Kingdom.

Figure 2.3 **Index-linked debt in OECD countries, 2008-2018**

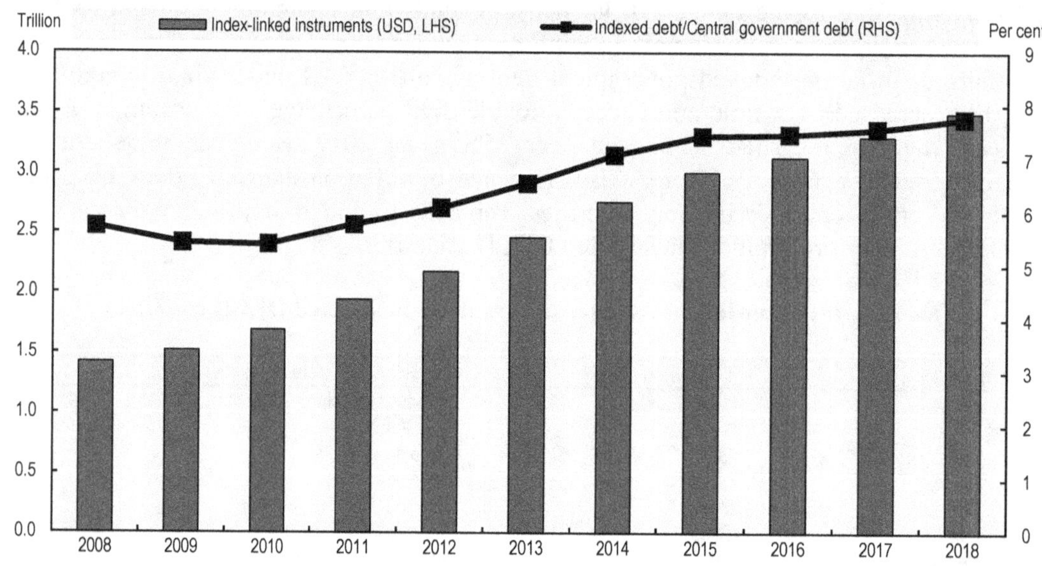

Notes: Values of marketable index-linked debt and total central government marketable debt have been aggregated by using fixed exchange rates, as of 1st December 2009, for all years.

Source: 2017 Survey on Central Government Marketable Debt and Borrowing carried out by the OECD Working Party on Debt Management; OECD Economic Outlook No. 102; Thomson Reuters, national authorities' websites and author calculations.

StatLink http://dx.doi.org/10.1787/888933689672

Figure 2.4 **Country breakdown of outstanding index-linked bonds in 2017**

As a percentage of central government debt

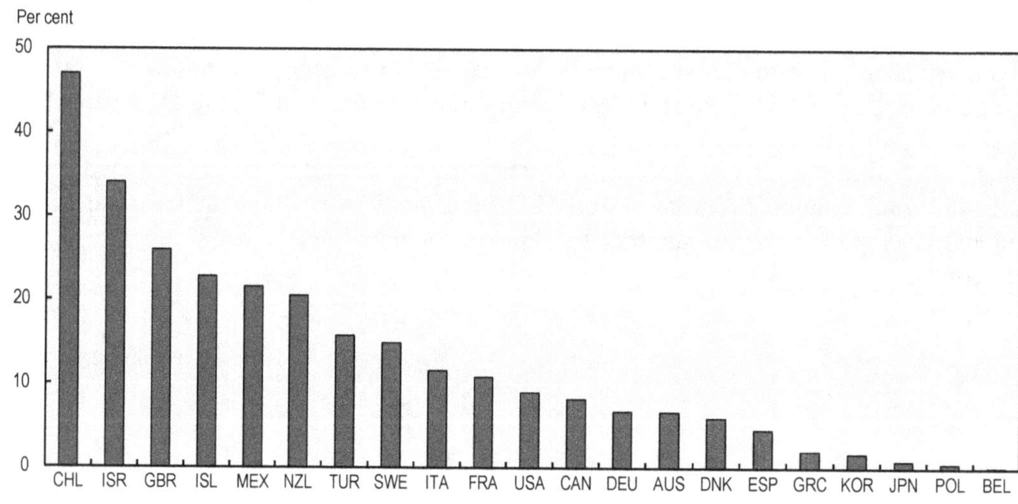

Source: 2017 Survey on Central Government Marketable Debt and Borrowing carried out by the OECD Working Party on Debt Management; Thomson Reuters, national authorities' websites and author calculations.

StatLink http://dx.doi.org/10.1787/888933689691

Reviewing different country experiences, Shen (2009) argues that the experience highlights the crucial role of market liquidity, although such liquidity may be more difficult to achieve than in markets for conventional nominal bonds. He notes that, while issuers have experience with different forms of structures and indexation for their inflation-linkers (for an overview, see Box 3.1 of *Sovereign Borrowing Outlook* 2017), a fairly common structure emerged, as follows: The principal is indexed to grow at the same rate as an index of prices, while the coupon rate is fixed at issuance. As the nominal coupon is obtained by multiplying the fixed coupon rate by the nominal principal, the former grows at the same rate as the price index. Similarly, at maturity, the amount being repaid is the sum of the initial principal at par and the accumulated growth in the nominal principal, due to realised increases in the inflation index. There seems to be an advantage in providing fairly simple structures for debt instruments. That said, despite this fairly common structure, a liquidity concession tends to prevail in the case of inflation-linkers as compared to conventional nominal bonds as the latter are traded more often and as part of hedging strategies, given their benchmark status, while the former tend also to be bought to a larger extent by buy-and-hold investors. The liquidity premium tends to decline over time as more experience accumulates with a new inflation-linker programme. These experiences are useful reference points when considering the introduction of new "non-standard" sovereign debt instruments e.g. contingent bonds with payments linked to GDP developments, as discussed in the next section. Although an important caveat is that the inflation-linked product has met with considerable investor demand, which may not be the case for some untested alternative instruments.

2.5 Proposals for considering issuance of GDP-linked sovereign bonds

Against the background of historically high levels of sovereign debt in many OECD countries, proposals to consider issuing sovereign debt instruments, whose repayments are indexed to domestic GDP, have received renewed attention. Some central banks including the Bank of England, Bank of Canada, and the Banque de France have explored the economic potential of such instruments, although no OECD government has sought to issue such bonds in practice. The main theoretical advantage of this kind of debt is that it could limit the variation of the debt-to-GDP ratio, and hence the risk of a debt crisis and costly debt renegotiations. Conceptually, when real economic activity turns out to be weak so that tax revenues are relatively low, GDP-indexed bonds (depending on how they were structured) could pay a low coupon, and hence allow the sovereign issuer to save on debt-servicing costs. Currently, OECD public debt levels are at post-World War II highs and the real activity outlook, while slightly improving, remains uncertain. Against this background, the OECD Committee on Financial Markets discussed the idea that such instruments could complement the stock of more traditional sovereign debt instruments.

A main conceptual advantage of GDP-linked bonds is that sovereign debt sustainability would be enhanced. A wider range of risk management tools would become available and financial market resilience would be fostered as the transfer of specific types of macroeconomic risks to investors willing to bear such risks is facilitated. From an investor perspective, exposure to GDP developments, acquired through the purchase of such bonds, could provide diversification benefits that might be higher than those gained through stock index investments for any given country. This stems from the observation that nominal growth in USD is usually less volatile and less correlated with standard financial portfolios than are equity returns, thus implying better diversification gains from investments in GDP-linked bonds than in local stock market indices (Cabrillac et. al., 2016).

Benford et. al,. (2017) distinguish between potential issuance during "normal times" and (periods of) debt restructurings. In normal times, GDP-linked bonds could theoretically offer additional fiscal space in downturns, another way of deleveraging from high debt levels and a way of reducing the risk of solvency crises. If achievable, these benefits would be likely to be largest when debt levels are already high relative to GDP and there is a non-trivial probability of debt reaching an unsustainable trajectory, although it may be difficult or costly to transfer such risks to investors. In debt restructurings, GDP-linked bonds could theoretically help by back-loading debt repayments to when recovery is fully underway and help governments insure themselves against subsequent negative growth shocks and having to restructure again. In fact, however, all GDP-index-linked instruments that have been issued so far are warrants that only give the investor participation in the upside risk, and were issued as part of debt restructurings. Examples include; Argentina (2005 and 2010), Greece (2012) and Ukraine (2015). In these cases, instruments were issued as part of sovereign debt restructurings, which extend for 20 years or more and that foresee contingent upside payments to investors either tied to real GDP growth or levels (for an overview see IMF, 2017). These securities did not foresee any fall in payments to investors in the event of a downside scenario.

Discussions by the Committee on Financial Markets highlighted that, despite the conceptual attractiveness of GDP-linked bonds, issuance of such bonds faces numerous practical challenges, which explains why such instruments have so far not become part of regular issuance during normal times in advanced economies. Questions arise in particular as regards to the investor base for such instruments, the cost-effectiveness of such issuance and market pricing.

As compared to conventional bonds,[3] two additional factors can affect the risk premium that applies to GDP-indexed bonds. In addition to a liquidity and credit risk premium, a novelty and indexation premium characterise the latter. The novelty premium can be expected to disappear and the liquidity premium to be further compressed if this type of bond becomes more firmly established as part of the range of sovereign debt instruments, but this would depend on there being sustained interest from an investor base. Such a development was observed in the case of other contingent sovereign bonds such as inflation linkers, as discussed in the previous section. The indexation (or growth risk) premium compensates investors for the greater volatility in total return. This premium reflects uncertainty about GDP developments and the level of the premium charged to compensate for that uncertainty. The Committee on Financial Markets (CMF) agreed that this premium remained a key issue.

At the same time, many CMF delegates expected to see the novelty and liquidity premium decline with time and amounts issued. Also, the default risk premium could play a mitigating role but only to the extent that such a significant part of public debt is issued in the form of GDP-linked bonds that public debt would credibly become more sustainable. Carnot and Pamies Sumner (2017) illustrate that the fall in the probability of explosive debt paths could lower the default risk premium considerably, both on conventional and on GDP-linked debt as compared to conventional debt, for countries within a monetary union. The Committee suggested that the net effect in terms of risk premiums after issuance of GDP-indexed bonds, both on such bonds and on conventional bonds, depends however not only on issuance volumes but on the specific characteristics of each country. In fact, there is considerable uncertainty regarding the total premium on GDP-linked bonds as compared to conventional bonds and a high risk premium could undo some or all of the expected conceptual benefits of GDP-linked bonds. Not enough is known about potential investor demand for such bonds.

2.5.1. Debt managers' views on GDP-linked bonds

The 2017 survey circulated among OECD DMOs revealed that none of the respondent countries has considered issuance of GDP-linked instruments to be appropriate. While some recognise that the theoretical counter-cyclical feature of GDP-linked bonds is appealing, there are strong concerns about the GDP-linked bonds as an instrument for sovereign borrowing due to the following factors: i) existence of natural investor base is unclear, as well as sustainability of demand; ii) lack of established standard; iii) higher cost because of the novelty of the product and the lack of natural demand, the small market size; iv) the uncertainty of cash flows; and v) regular – and sometimes significant – revisions of GDP data.

In light of the survey results, members of the OECD Working Party on Public Debt Management (WPDM) discussed various policy and operational aspects of GDP-linked instruments during their 2017 annual meeting. Debt managers acknowledged potential macroeconomic benefits associated with GDP-linked instruments. Nevertheless, they highlighted the existence of substantial constraints in terms of investor base, financing costs and pricing. From the debt managers' perspective, it is extremely difficult and costly to develop a market for a new instrument and also continue to implement a predictable government financing programme in the absence of a robust and viable investor demand. In this respect, they noted that, unlike inflation-linked bonds for which pension funds and insurance companies are considered natural investors, the existence of a natural investor base is unclear for GDP-linked instruments. Furthermore, from an investor perspective, hedging against growth volatility may not be attractive as a lot of uncertainty exists around the projection of GDP. Debt managers also added that operational complexities related to indexation and regular revisions of GDP data can make it difficult to develop liquidity for this instrument, even if the initial novelty premium may slowly fade away as the stock of new instrument grows.

2.6 A rising prospect for green bonds

Green bonds are simply debt instruments used to finance green projects that deliver environmental benefits (OECD, 2017a). In terms of financial features, a green bond does not deliver a different cash flow than that of a typical conventional bond. In this regard, there is nothing unusual from a pure fixed income perspective about green bonds. However, the use of proceeds from green bonds, and pre- and post-issuance reporting requirements, are very different from conventional bonds.

The green bond market, which started with multinational organisations' issuance (including EIB, IFC and the World Bank) over a decade ago, has deepened and expanded with a diversified issuer profile, including various corporate entities and local governments. On the demand side, the number of investors who are committed to responsible investment and integrating environmental, social and governance factors into their investment processes is increasing quite rapidly (e.g. Norwegian Global Fund, Denmark's ATP Pension Fund, Swedish National Pension Fund and The California State Teachers' Retirement System etc.),[4] which, in turn, supports portfolio investments in green securities. In the light of growing demand, the volume of green bond issuance has increased significantly. The OECD report 'Mobilising Bond Markets for a Low-Carbon Transition' estimates that annual issuance of "green bonds" rose from USD 3 billion in 2011 to USD 95 billion in 2016 (OECD, 2017a). The report concludes that there is a strong potential for green bonds to develop as a means of channelling finance and savings towards environmental projects and, in turn, to become a significant fixed income asset class over the next decade, in the light of increasing attention to climate risks and opportunities in investment portfolios.

While corporate bonds have dominated the universe of green financing so far (with a 60% share), a few sovereign issuers have entered the green bond market recently. In the OECD area, Poland and France became pioneers in the sovereign green bond market with their green bond launches, in December 2016 and January 2017 respectively. Following these successful offerings, Malaysia (in July 2017)[5] and Fiji (in October 2017) also issued green securities. In January 2018, Belgium issued its inaugural green bond with 15 year maturity.

The bonds issued during the past two years by Belgium, France and Poland are inspired by the Green Bond Principles (GBP) and profited from a positive market story recently. The GBP, updated as of June 2017 by the International Capital Market Association (ICMA),[6] sets the main standards associated with the green bond issuance process. The GBP recommends transparency and disclosure to promote integrity in development of the green market. Following these principles, French and Polish DMOs attached special importance to reporting requirements associated with the government projects financed through green bonds. With respect to their recent experience, both countries noted the following among the main challenges with issuing green bonds: (1) ex-ante reporting requirements and ex-post impact assessment, (2) coordination among relevant parties, and (3) special marketing events, including organisation of roadshows.

Specifically, the French Treasury's inaugural issuance of green bonds, the proceeds of which are used to fund a group of green expenditures, sets a good example in terms of: i) the choice of maturity segment and of green eligible budget expenditure; ii) the establishment of a green evaluation council for ex-post impact assessment; and iii) fair pricing of the bond in comparison with existing bonds with similar maturities (Box 2.1). Furthermore, the French Treasury is committed to the green market, meaning that green bond issuance will be a regular part of the issuance programme in the future.

The survey on 'Alternative Approaches to Sovereign Borrowing' asks sovereign debt managers' views on a number of potential barriers to green bond issuance, the results of which are presented in *Figure 2.5*. Of the 31 respondents, 22 countries emphasised the cost of specific requirements as a major entry-barrier. Although green bonds display similar cash flow projections to conventional bonds, they require issuers to perform distinctive monitoring and reporting activities in order to adapt green standards, along with additional marketing events to reach out to new investors. Also, budgetary rules might pose an impediment for sovereign issuers, since earmarked budget financing is prohibited by law from supporting fiscal discipline in several OECD countries. In such cases, it is essential for governments to make appropriate adjustments in the legislative framework to enable earmarking of funds for specific projects (e.g. Poland)[7]. All of these specific requirements, in turn, bring about additional transaction/operation costs for issuers. However, issuers identify that some of the costs and difficulties are only related to the initial issuance process.

According to the survey results, more than 20% of respondents gave high scores to 'lack of standards and reference guidelines', 'rarity of sovereign issues' and 'lack of green government expenditure to finance', as challenges associated with a green bond issuance. Also, results indicate that sovereign debt managers assess demand-side factors (i.e. 'lack of investor demand', 'dominance of buy-and-hold type of investors' and 'scarcity of green bond funds and indices') as posing less of a challenge than those presented by the first two entry-barriers.

Box 2.1. **Sovereign green bonds:**
Case study of the French Treasury's inaugural issuance

In January 2017, the French DMO (Agence France Trésor, AFT) launched the first French sovereign green bond with a 22-year maturity and a total size of EUR 7 billion by syndication technique. The motive for issuing the green bond is indicated to support the implementation of the Paris Climate Agreement under the terms of the Energy Transition and Green Growth Act. As such, central government budget expenditure and expenditure under the "Invest for the Future" programme to fight climate change, adapt to climate change, protect biodiversity and fight pollution will be funded by a green bond (also referred to as Green OAT 'Obligation Assimilable du Trésor').

Before issuing the Green OAT, the AFT designed a comprehensive framework based on the 'Green Bond Principles' and the 'Transition Energétique et Ecologique pour le Climat' (TEEC) label. The framework includes the following key features:

- *Process for project evaluation and selection:* The screening is made by an inter-ministerial working group coordinated by the Ministry of Finance and the Ministry of Environment, under the supervision of the Prime Minister. A 'Green OAT Evaluation Council', made up of independent scientists and economists, evaluates ex-post the environmental performance of France's Eligible Green Expenditures.

- *Management of proceeds:* The proceeds from the green bond are managed in compliance with the general budget rule and finance an equivalent amount of Eligible Green Expenditure. In practice, the proceeds of the Green OAT are treated similarly to those of a conventional bond, but the allocations to Eligible Green Expenditure will be tracked and reported.

- *Monitoring and reporting:* Two annual reports are to be published for investors until full allocation of the funds: (i) a report on the use of proceeds and (ii) a report on the performance of 'Eligible Green Expenditure'. In addition, the ex-post environmental impact of 'Eligible Green Expenditure' is to be evaluated in a special report at appropriate intervals, under the supervision of the Green OAT Evaluation Council, which contributes to setting high standards in green bond market.

The AFT is committed to enhancing liquidity of the green OAT by successive tap issues. It is stated that the proceeds from tap issues will also be matched to 'Eligible Green Expenditure', as the cumulative amount of such expenditure rises over the coming years.

Source: Agence France Trésor (AFT), www.aft.gouv.fr

Figure 2.5. **Assessing barriers to green bond issuance**

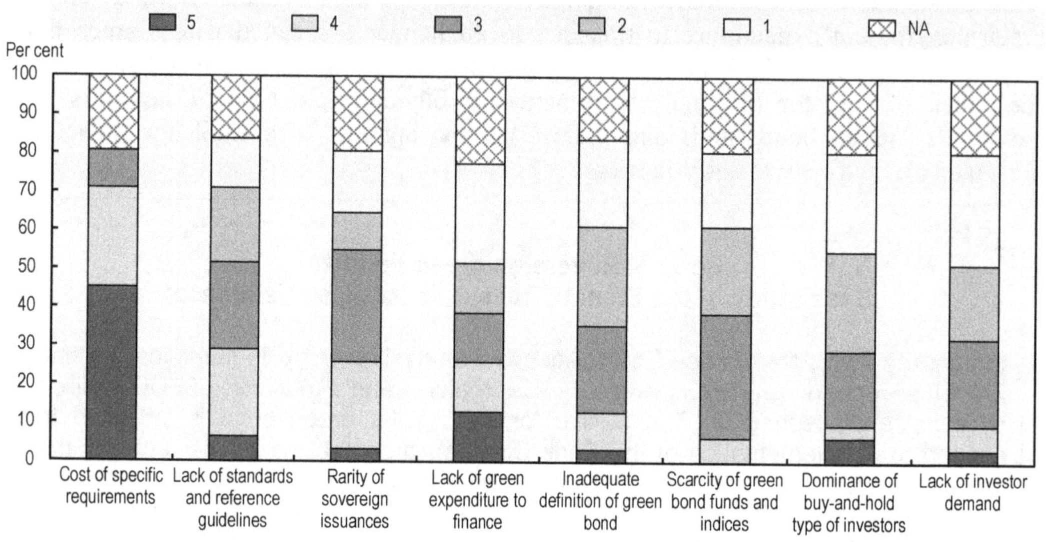

Notes: Respondents were asked to score on a scale from 1 to 5, where 1 = no significance and 5 = very significant. Respondents were free to replicate scores for different barriers.

Source: 2017 Survey on Alternative Approaches to Sovereign Borrowing, carried out by the OECD Working Party on Debt Management.

StatLink *http://dx.doi.org/10.1787/888933689710*

2.7 Experiences with sukuk issuance

Sukuk, an Islamic finance instrument, is defined as "certificates of equal value representing undivided shares in ownership of tangible assets, usufruct and services or (in the ownership of) the assets of particular projects or special investment activity" (AAOIFI, 2008). According to Islamic finance, investors should receive a return from the profits of their investment where they have pro-rata ownership rights to the underlying assets, not simply for the provision of money (i.e. riba, or interest). In this regard, and different from conventional debt instruments, sukuk issuance pre-requisites transfer of ownership or usage benefits on an underlying asset, and adherence to Islamic Law (Sharia). Therefore, governments, especially in non-Islamic jurisdictions, need to adopt a special legal framework to accommodate Islamic finance in order to launch sukuk (Balibek E., 2017). Based on the project to be financed, there are different types of sukuk certificates including 'Ijara', 'Murabaha', 'Istisna' and 'Musharaka'. Among the list of various sukuk contracts, the most common type is ijara (leasing) sukuk which generates a stream of financial income for investors through leasing of tangible asset(s).

In terms of the investor base, in addition to retail investors who are against interest earnings, institutional investors, such as sovereign wealth funds from Middle Eastern countries and Islamic investment banks, have been active in structuring their investments in sukuk market. Given this strong and sustainable investor demand, the sukuk market has attracted various issuers within and outside of the Islamic world since the early 1990s. Global sukuk outstanding reached USD 320 billion in 2016 (IFSB, 2017). Sovereign issues accounted for approximately 80% (USD 75 billion) of the total sukuk issuance in 2016, of which Malaysia represented more than 50% of the market (IFSB, 2017).

In the OECD area, three countries, namely Luxembourg, Turkey and the United Kingdom, experienced sovereign sukuk issuance. Sukuk practice in the OECD area is limited to ijara (lease) structure due to its simplicity, tradability and ability to provide a fixed flow of income for investors.[8] Luxembourg and the United Kingdom, who both issued sovereign ijara sukuk in 2014 via the syndication method, indicated respectively that 'being innovative' and 'supporting finance centre' were the main motivations for standalone issuance. In the case of Turkey, 'diversifying borrowing instruments' and 'broadening the investor base' were the major factors driving the sukuk programme. It should be noted that among OECD countries, Turkey where a majority of the population is Muslim, is the only country where sukuk is part of the regular funding programme.

The Turkish Treasury, the institution in charge of sovereign debt management, executed its first sovereign sukuk issuance in 2012, following the enactment of amendments to existing legislation. Since then, the Treasury has issued inflation-indexed lease certificates along with fixed leasing certificates[9] for local and foreign investors who are reluctant to invest in interest-bearing securities. Recently, Turkey embarked on another innovative sukuk issuance called 'gold-indexed lease certificate'. Through this new instrument, the authorities were aiming at traditional investors to channel their idle gold holdings into financial markets and to raise low saving rates in the economy (Turkish Treasury, 2017). In 2017, the share of sukuk in government borrowing reached 3% of outstanding government debt in Turkey.

Regarding difficulties experienced with sukuk issuance, all three issuers indicated a high legal cost along with additional administrative costs attached. Legal costs refer to the cost of changes in existing legislation or creating stand-alone laws in order to comply with Islamic finance rules, and specialist structuring advice and requirements. Additional administrative costs arise because the issuance process requires a selection of available tangible assets, such as government buildings and land, as well as numerous transactions of these assets between government entities.

Country responses to the survey also emphasised the cost of specific requirements associated with sukuk. Specifically, a few countries have considered issuing a sukuk but – for the moment – decided against issuance and noted that the complexity of a sukuk transaction, additional costs including legislative changes, and lack of local investor demand were the major obstacles.

2.8 Opportunities and obstacles of ultra-long bond issuance

Ultra-long bonds (ULB) are similar to traditional bonds, except for their maturity profile. ULB issuance has been increasing in recent years, although they are not part of sovereign issuance programmes in the majority of OECD countries. Indeed, in some countries, there are legal limits to the maximum maturity of sovereign bonds. For example, in Portugal, maturity of a borrowing instrument is limited to 50 years by law. Austria, which launched 70-year tenor in 2016 and 100-year tenor in 2017, has changed the legal framework to allow issuance up to 100 years.

Survey results on ULBs revealed that 14 OECD countries have issued ULBs from 40 to 100-year maturity. In terms of issuance volume of ULBs, four countries (Canada, Korea, Ireland and Switzerland) mentioned no commitment to ensuring liquidity while eight countries commit to ensuring liquidity through the usual measures existing for traditional bonds (re-openings, market making obligations, etc.). *Figure 2.6* reflects aggregate figures for government issuance of ultra-long bonds. Compared to pre-crisis years, government ultra-long bond issuances have increased significantly since 2009 as a result of increased borrowing requirements, as well as maturity choice in issuance strategy. By issuing ULBs, DMOs aim mainly for lengthening the debt portfolio duration and reducing refinancing risk, as well as taking advantage of a low yield environment. As discussed in Chapter 1 of this publication, most DMOs have been able to extend the average length of their public debt in recent years. Historical evolution of the average term-to-maturity of outstanding central government debt, as an imperfect proxy for refinancing risk exposure, indicates a 1.5-year increase compared to the pre-crisis period.

Figure 2.6. **Issuance of government bonds with longer than 30-year maturities**

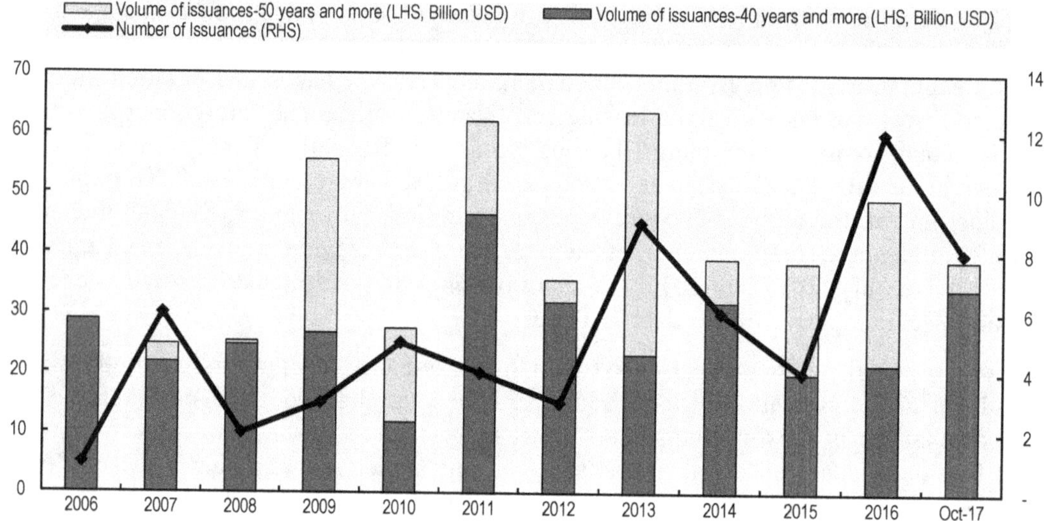

Notes: OECD countries only. Volume is based on issuance amounts using flexible exchange rates. Annual cumulative totals in each year, except for 2017 where the cumulative total is up to October 2017.

Source: Thomson Reuters, national authorities' websites and author calculations.

StatLink ⧉ http://dx.doi.org/10.1787/888933689729

During the past two years, Austria, Belgium and Ireland have issued 100-year bonds, also referred to as 'century bonds'. Issuing a century bond is usually considered as a sign of strong market confidence for investors. Also, another incentive for creating an ultra-long benchmark is for valuation of long-term projects (e.g. Austria), in addition to lengthening the portfolio duration and reducing refinancing risk.

In the absence of a benchmark bond, it is difficult for issuers to grasp investors' appetite and bid pricing level before committing to a transaction. Indeed, survey results indicate that, except for a few countries (e.g. Canada, Japan, Switzerland and the United Kingdom) – where ULBs are part of regular funding programme –, issuers of ULBs have concerns about pricing since a benchmark bond in several cases did not exist. In general, the inaugural issuance is completed through syndication or private placement. The bond is then tapped via auctions (e.g. Austria, France, Italy, Korea and Spain) due to several reasons, including stronger primary dealer (PD) motivation to perform, flexibility in terms of timing (independent of the auction calendar) and easier price discovery during book-building in the syndication process.

Based on survey results, various issues surrounding this topic were discussed during the last annual meeting of the OECD WPDM, held 2-3 November in 2017. Debt managers acknowledged potential benefits and risks associated with issuance of ultra-long bonds. Long-term debt issuance, and ultra long-term debt in particular, provides predictability of redemptions over decades in advance. Debt managers benefit from long-term bond issuances to diversify a government's debt portfolio and reduce maturity mismatches on the sovereign balance sheet, as well as to mitigate refinancing risk of the outstanding debt. The majority of issuers noted that bonds with longer than 30-year maturities are tactical decisions to lock in historically low interest rates and rapidly reduce re-financing risk.

Some sovereign debt managers are cautious about the depth and sustainability of investor demand for ULBs, particularly after the exit from unconventional monetary policies. In the absence of continued demand, ultra-long issuance might be opportunistic and inconsistent with regular and predictable financing policies. The natural investor base consists of insurance companies and pension funds,[10] which could match ultra-long bonds to their ultra-long liabilities. As suggested by Domanski, D. et al. (2017), declining long-term interest rates are likely to widen the negative duration gap between the assets and liabilities of insurers and pension funds; this, in turn, tends to increase portfolio managers' demand for long-term bonds as an attempt to contain asset-liability mismatches. In addition to liability-driven investors, much of the recent demand for long-term bonds is driven by a broader spectrum of investors searching for positive yields.

Against this backdrop, most countries that have issued ULBs consider that demand looks sustainable for the 40- and, 50-year segment, mainly due to a structural demand from insurers and pension funds, and the attractive features of ULBs: higher yield, convexity and long-dated asset / liability matching. It was noted that the end of Public Sector Purchase Programme (PSPP) in Europe is not expected to make a difference with regard to ULBs as they are not in the scope of the purchase programme. In Japan, 40-year bonds were already introduced before Bank of Japan engaged in unconventional monetary policy. Nevertheless, debt managers assessed that investor demand for 100-year bonds may not be as strong as the 40- or, 50-year segment after the exit from unconventional monetary policies.

Countries which have not considered issuing ULBs mentioned the need to maintain liquidity on traditional bonds, the lack of sustainable demand, cost considerations, and had the opinion that it is ethically wrong to move debt burdens to future generations. In this regard, one of the issues related to ULBs is the risk of fragmenting market liquidity at the long end of the yield curve. When a large group of investors shift from one existing maturity segment to a new one, this development deteriorates market liquidity for the existing segment. Therefore, potential issuers consider that the presence of a strong and sustainable investor demand for ULBs is essential to avoid potential cannibalisation of other long-term bonds, particularly 30-year tenor and 'orphan' issues that might be trading poorly. That said, in general, most ULB issuance so far has generally had no big impact on other maturity segments, as issuance has been quite limited.

Notes

1.   In the context of sovereign debt management, 'natural investor base" is often used to refer to a group of investors who has an investment objective biasing them towards investing in a particular bond segment.

2. The difference between the nominal yield on a fixed-coupon bond and the real yield on an index-linked bond with similar maturity is often referred to as the breakeven inflation rate.

3. It is understood that robust contracts are needed to mitigate investor concerns and limit the potential of such premia to undermine the potential theoretical benefits of GDP-linked bonds. A working group, led by the Bank of England, has developed a "London Term Sheet" for GDP-linked bonds; it is available at www.icmagroup.org/resources/Sovereign-Debt-Information/ and is summarised in Box 7 of IMF (2017).

4. In 2016, a Swedish pension fund established a dedicated green bond portfolio, arguing that the market has "achieved a maturity and size" to justify the fund implementing a separate investment strategy and classifying its green bond holdings as a distinct asset class.

5. The Malaysian government issued the first green sukuk bond in July 2017.

6. The Green Bond Principles by ICMA: www.icmagroup.org/Regulatory-Policy-and-Market-Practice/green-bonds/green-bond-principles

7. In France where earmarked financing is prohibited, the Treasury used a "nominal equivalence approach" in terms of green expenditure and bond proceeds, and committed adequate reporting.

8. While Ijara is the most preferred form of sukuk type, due to simplicity, tradability and ability to provide a fixed flow of income for investors, the issuance process requires several complex transactions among government agencies, including the DMO, Special Purpose Vehicle and Ministry of Finance (Balibek, E. 2017).

9. Lease Certificates are securities that are issued by the Undersecretariat of the Treasury Asset Leasing Company (UTALC) in order to finance the assets acquired or leased. These certificates grant investors with entitlements to revenues generated from such assets in proportion to their shares.

10. Demand from pension funds for ULBs partially depends on the pension system. For example, in the United Kingdom and Canada where demand for ULBs is strong, pension funds are – still - dominantly based on a defined benefit (DB) system. However, the low and falling interest rate environment and increasing longevity risks in recent years haveed to a decline in the importance of DB plans. A rapid shift to defined contribution retirement plans from DB plans in countries (e.g. the United States) would imply a reduction in demand for ULBs.

References

AAOIFI (2008), *"Sharia Standards for Financial Institutions"*, Accounting and Auditing Organization for Islamic Financial Institutions, Bahrain; http://aaoifi.com/standard/shariah-standards/?lang=en

Benford, J., Thomas Best and Mark Joy, Bank of England, with contributions from Mark Kruger, Bank of Canada, and the Research Department, Central Bank of Argentina, Bank of England, Financial Stability Paper No. 39 – September, 2016; www.bankofengland.co.uk/financialstability/Documents/fpc/fspapers/fs_paper39.pdf

Balibek, Emre (2017), "Establishing a Legal Framework for Sovereign Sukuk Issuance", World Bank Discussion Paper, June 2017, No.18, Washington DC;

http://documents.worldbank.org/curated/en/907001497472893193/pdf/P161573-06-14-2017-1497472889089.pdf

Carnot, N. and S. Pamies Sumner (2017), "GDP-linked bonds: Some simulations on EU countries", European Commission Discussion Paper 073, December 2017; https://ec.europa.eu/info/publications/economy-finance/gdp-linked-bonds-some-simulations-eu-countries_en

Domanski, D., H. S. Shin and V. Sushko (2017), "The Hunt for Duration: Not Waving but Drowning?", IMF Economic Review Vol. 65, No. 1 October 2017; https://www.imf.org/external/np/res/seminars/2015/arc/pdf/Domanski.pdf

French Treasury (2017), "Framework for the Green OAT", January 2017, Agence France Trésor, Paris,; www.aft.gouv.fr/documents/%7BC3BAF1F0-F068-4305-821D-B8B2BF4F9AF6%7D/publication/attachments/25562.pdf

ICMA (2017), *Green Bond Principles,* International Capital Market Association June 2017; https://www.icmagroup.org/assets/documents/Regulatory/Green-Bonds/GreenBondsBrochure-JUNE2017.pdf

IMF (2017), "IMF Policy Paper – State-contingent debt instruments for sovereigns", May 2017; https://www.imf.org/en/About/Key-Issues/state-contingent-debt-instruments

Islamic Financial Services Board (2017), "Islamic Financial Services Industry Stability Report 2017", May 2017, Kuala Lumpur; www.ifsb.org/docs/IFSB%20IFSI%20Stability%20Report%202017.pdf

OECD (2017a), *Mobilising Bond Markets for a Low-Carbon Transition*, OECD Publishing, Paris; http://dx.doi.org/10.1787/9789264272323-en

OECD (2016), *OECD Sovereign Borrowing Outlook 2016*, OECD Publishing, Paris; http://dx.doi.org/10.1787/sov_b_outlk-2016-en

OECD (2017b), *OECD Sovereign Borrowing Outlook 2017*, OECD Publishing, Paris. http://dx.doi.org/10.1787/sov_b_outlk-2017-en

Shen, P. (2009), Federal Reserve Bank of Kansas City Economic Review, First Quarter 2009; www.kansascityfed.org/publicat/econrev/pdf/3q95shen.pdf

Thedéen, Erik (2004), "Ten years with inflation-linked bonds – a new asset class has been established", Speech by Deputy Director General of the Swedish National Debt Office at a seminar organised by FIM Asset Management Ltd on 12 May 2004 in Helsinki, Finland; https://www.riksgalden.se/globalassets/dokument_eng/press/speeches/upl855-realhelsinki_eng_040512.pdf

Turkish Treasury Financing Program (2017), "2017 Developments and 2018 Projections", Press Release on 31 October 2017, Undersecretariat of Treasury, Ankara Turkey; www.treasury.gov.tr/public-finance-announcements

ANNEX 2.A1

Methods and sources

Calculations, definitions and data sources

- The OECD area denotes the following 35 countries: Australia, Austria, Belgium, Canada, Chile, Czech Republic, Denmark, Estonia, Finland, France, Germany, Greece, Hungary, Iceland, Ireland, Israel, Italy, Japan, Korea, Latvia, Luxembourg, Mexico, Netherlands, New Zealand, Norway, Poland, Portugal, Slovak Republic, Slovenia, Spain, Sweden, Switzerland, Turkey, the United Kingdom and the United States.

- To facilitate comparisons with previous versions of the Outlook, figures are converted into US dollars using exchange rates from 1 December 2009, unless indicated otherwise. Where figures are converted into US dollars using flexible exchange rates, the main text refers explicitly to that approach. Source: Thomson Reuters. The effects of using alternative exchange rate assumptions (in particular, fixing the exchange rate versus using flexible exchange rates) are illustrated in Figures 1.3 and 1.4 of Chapter 1 of the *Sovereign Borrowing Outlook, 2016*.

- All figures refer to calendar years unless specified otherwise.

- Aggregate figures for index-linked debt are compiled from answers to the Borrowing Survey. In cases of missing information for 2017 and/or 2018, the OECD Secretariat inserted its own estimates/projections using publicly available official information on redemptions and central government budget balances.

Chapter 3

A public debt management perspective on liquidity in sovereign bond markets

In recent years market participants in several jurisdictions have become increasingly concerned about government securities markets becoming less liquid over time. Changes in market liquidity may reflect a variety of factors, including: unconventional monetary policies; financial sector adjustments to post-crisis regulations; changes in composition of the investor base, and the proliferation of electronic trading venues and strategies.

The secondary market liquidity of government bonds is of utmost importance for sovereign debt managers, as this is an important contributing factor in supporting primary market access and minimising sovereign borrowing costs. Sovereign debt managers regularly monitor and review liquidity in government securities markets, based on a range of quantitative and qualitative data. Debt Management Offices benefit greatly from operationally and informationally efficient markets, and often play a key role in developing and securing well-functioning markets. In case of an illiquidity concern, sovereign debt managers take proactive – and sometimes innovative – steps to address potential risks associated with deteriorating market liquidity. This chapter presents empirical findings on liquidity conditions in selected government markets in recent years and the views of sovereign debt managers on structural changes affecting market liquidity, including measures taken to improve liquidity conditions.

3.1 Introduction

The previous edition of the *Outlook (2017)* highlighted sovereign debt managers' concerns about liquidity conditions in government bond markets. This chapter takes an in-depth look at the issue, supported by empirical evidence based on 2017 OECD survey of liquidity in secondary government bond markets, with a special focus on selected country practices and policy tools in addressing liquidity concerns.

Key findings

- Any development that impairs liquidity of bond markets reduces primary market access and increases sovereign borrowing costs. Hence, sovereign debt managers have a vital interest and a great responsibility in continuous, well-functioning government debt markets. In addition, market liquidity for government securities, a fundamental part of financial market structure, is an important element of supporting financial stability.

- Debt managers take actions and implement policies in order to promote efficiency in the government securities market. Being a transparent and predictable issuer helps Debt Management Offices (DMOs) reassure investors that the instruments on demand will be available, and enables them to plan out their investment strategy, thereby increasing the attractiveness of government bond markets.

- Sovereign debt managers actively monitor market developments and identify sources of stress, based on a range of data including relative market liquidity measures like spreads, trade volumes and price volatility. Therefore, DMOs need to have access to sufficient information to perform secondary market monitoring.

- A recent survey of liquidity in secondary government bond markets revealed that sovereign debt managers have continued to express worries about a perceived decline in liquidity in a variety of markets, albeit less than in previous years. The survey highlights the main driving factors affecting liquidity as financial sector adjustments to the post-crisis regulatory reforms, central banks purchasing programmes, as well as developments associated with market infrastructures.

- While advances in trading technology generate new prospects, including the potential for quicker, safer and cheaper financial transactions, thereby delivering significant efficiencies for market participants, execution models such as automated trading have created a number of new threats related to cyber-security, algo malfunctions and other operational risks. Therefore, DMOs stress the importance of market participants carefully employing a strong internal risk control environment to deal with these risks, and a financial regulatory framework that keeps pace with the new market structure.

- DMOs have a wide range of tools in place to enhance the degree of liquidity in government securities markets, including a benchmark bond program, security lending facility and primary dealership system. In response to recent concerns, debt managers in some countries, including Denmark and Turkey, have modified obligations and privileges of primary dealers to enhance their role in secondary market activities.

3.2 The importance of secondary market liquidity for sovereign debt managers

Government securities play a critical and unique role in local financial markets in every country. Besides financing government budget deficits, government securities help financial institutions to manage their risks, provide benchmarks for other financial instruments, facilitate the implementation of monetary policy and offer savers both individual and institutional, a low-risk, liquid and reliable investment. Unlike their corporate counterparts, government securities have a wider role in the financial system due to their "risk-free" status. In addition to being an instrument in portfolio management, they are widely used as collateral to secure financing through loans and repo markets[1] or to make margin payments against derivative transactions. The presence of high credit quality and liquid collaterals eases investors' transaction exposure, which in turn facilitates their financing cost conditions (Das *et al.,* 2010). Also, private sector funding in an economy is benchmarked to government bonds as the sovereign yield curve serves as a reference point for pricing other instruments, such as corporate bonds and loans.

Given the significance of their size and role, the government securities market is strongly interconnected to other components of the local financial system. Hence, market liquidity for government securities, a fundamental part of the financial market structure, is an important element of financial stability. In times of stress, illiquid markets are subject to violent changes in asset prices, which may lead to substantial losses for financial institutions. From an investor's perspective, the degree of liquidity is an important trading criteria for a security, reflecting the ability to be easily bought or sold without a large price impact. As suggested by Keynes' liquidity preference theory, all other factors being equal, investors prefer securities with higher liquidity.

Market liquidity has important implications from a public debt management perspective: Reduced liquidity of government securities impairs – to some extent – the price discovery process in the secondary market and translates into higher yields through a liquidity premium[2] in primary markets which, in turn, increases borrowing costs for sovereigns. On the whole, any development that impairs the liquidity of bond markets increases sovereign borrowing costs. It should be noted that even small changes in the interest rate paid on a sovereign bond can result in significant costs or savings to taxpayers. Against this backdrop, DMOs have a great interest in, and responsibility for, continuous, well-functioning government debt markets. Therefore, DMOs often play a key role in developing and securing well-functioning markets.

In light of the significance of market liquidity for achieving low funding costs, sovereign debt managers closely monitor financial market developments and maintain a regular dialogue with market participants. In fact, developing and maintaining an efficient market for government securities is often stated in legal frameworks as one of the key responsibilities of DMOs in several OECD countries. The OECD's annual survey shows that all OECD DMOs, except for Luxembourg, measure and monitor market liquidity on a regular and an ad-hoc basis, considering a wide range of indicators. Relative market liquidity measures, such as bid-ask spreads, trade volumes and price volatility, each strongly explain liquidity conditions in government bond markets and shifts in the type of demand at different parts of the curve. Based on the survey results, a summary of common methods for monitoring market liquidity is provided in **Box 3.1.**

Box 3.1. **Common methods used by DMOs for monitoring market liquidity**

The existence of liquid government securities facilitates the price discovery process, and lowers the cost of sovereign debt. In this regard, sovereign debt managers try to judge the state of changes that occur in market liquidity of sovereign bond markets by regularly monitoring (usually on a daily basis) the government securities market, based on a range of quantitative and qualitative data. Continued communication with market players, including feedback from primary dealers and central bankers, is the main source of qualitative information, while quantitative materials are gathered mainly through primary dealers and financial data vendors. It should be noted that particular sources and types of information may gain special importance as some characteristics of liquid markets change over time.

Qualitative information: Qualitative data contains views and anecdotal evidence about changing investor sentiment (or expectations) and behaviour that underpins secondary market developments. DMOs collect qualitative data from various stakeholders on a wide range of issues related to government securities markets, including opinions and advice on the implications of recent and/or potential policy changes, regulatory reforms and preferences of market participants for future issuance types and techniques. Regular and ad-hoc meetings with primary dealers (PDs) and other large investors is an important source of qualitative feedbacks for DMOs who may also conduct surveys to acquire market views on a particular topic. In addition, debt managers are often in close contact with financial sector authorities, including national central banks and stock markets.

Quantitative information (liquidity metrics): DMOs use a number of liquidity metrics to assess market dynamics. Since no single measure can fully capture the different aspects of liquidity, such as depth, tightness and resiliency, DMOs often consider a range of various metrics, as well as market-specific factors and developments when structuring a framework for monitoring secondary market liquidity. OECD country responses to the 2017 survey on liquidity in secondary government bond markets suggest that the following indicators* are the most commonly used by OECD DMOs:

- Bid-Ask spreads, which are the absolute difference in price between what buyers are willing to pay and what sellers are willing to accept for a security, measure price tightness, and thus reflect transaction costs in bond markets. A higher bid-ask spread indicates higher transaction costs and lower liquidity conditions.

- Trade volumes, in gross and average terms, provide information about the number and size of trades conducted in markets and help to capture market depth.

- Turnover ratios, a simple comparison of trading volume to the outstanding amount of a security, represent trading frequency. A high turnover ratio implies the existence of continuous pricing of a security.

- Issue size shows the amount available for trading. Sovereign debt managers often pursue a benchmark bond issuance policy to reach a significant issue size of a bond, in turn to benefit from a liquidity premium.

- Composition of holders provides information about changing bond ownership. Typically, institutional investors such as pension funds, insurance companies and monetary authorities are characterised as buy-and-hold types of investors. Therefore, their increased presence in a market implies lower trading figures; while a growing share of banks, mutual funds, hedge funds and ETFs implies a relatively higher degree of market liquidity. It should be stated that there is a trade-off between buy-and hold type of investors and more speculative investors. A broad and well-balanced investor base (majorty of traditional buy-and-hold) is important.

* There are other types of liquidity indicators focusing on different aspects of liquidity (e.g. price impact measures, market efficiency co-efficient and Amihud (2002) illiquidity measure) some of which might require niche data and advanced econometric techniques. DMOs are selective in utilising these indicators based on data availability as well as cost-benefit considerations.

Source: Responses to 2017 OECD survey of liquidity in secondary government bond markets (Annex B).

As availability of comprehensive trade data on a timely basis is crucial for monitoring and interpreting market dynamics, DMOs attach special importance to improving collection of trade data in terms of its scope, quality and frequency. While most DMOs regularly obtain aggregate level data from primary dealers – primarily for measuring PDs' performance – and financial data vendors, it is often a significant challenge to access more granular data on a timely basis, such as high-frequency transaction level data. High-frequency data enables a precise identification of intra-day abnormalities. During the 2016 annual meeting of the OECD Working Party on Public Debt Management (WPDM), members elaborated existing practices in collecting, accessing and reporting micro-data. Discussions highlighted that although data collection on bond trade activities has improved in recent years in most OECD countries, there is still a data gap, particularly in *i)* high-frequency transaction-level bond market data, and *ii)* investor type and geographical distribution, regarding both holdings and flow data. Although the growing use of electronic trading applications (e.g. high-frequency trading, algo-trading) is beneficial, it also poses a number of challenges to policymakers, including the need to monitor the effect on market liquidity and functioning. For example, faced with major constraints in readily available micro-level data following the flash-crash in the US Treasury market in October 2014, US authorities initiated a project to obtain such data through the Financial Industry Regulatory Authority by expanding the Trade Reporting and Compliance Engine ('TRACE') (SEC, 2016).

Among OECD countries, Canada uses a leading practice to monitor secondary markets as described here. The Bank of Canada, as part of its fiscal-agent activities in the area of debt management, designed a comprehensive database and developed a liquidity dashboard to track and review market liquidity metrics. Based on multiple secondary market data sources, a number of liquidity metrics are tracked and maintained for the cash market, repo market, futures and spreads market. In addition to common indicators, listed in **Box 3.1**, they closely track settlement fails in repo markets. They utilise high-frequency data (micro-data) from financial markets.

Typically, the main pillars of sovereign debt management in OECD countries are transparency, predictability, regularity, liquidity, and prudence. This approach allows for borrowing that is also supportive of a liquid and well-functioning government securities market. Being a transparent and predictable issuer helps DMOs reassure investors that the instruments on demand will be regularly available, and also allows investors to better plan out their investment strategy. In this context, it is crucial that all potential buyers of government securities are simultaneously provided with the same information, and that dealers and investors are treated fairly and equally (OECD, 2016). As such, secondary market prices should fully reflect all available information about government debt statistics, operations and policies at any point in time. This practice in turn contributes to the price discovery process and enables market participants to make more informed investment choices in government bond markets.

Also, debt managers carefully consider the impact of their policy choices on a wide range of operations, including design of a debt issuance strategy, auction calendar, auction mechanisms and issuance procedures on bond market liquidity, and will adjust their strategies according to market conditions if deemed necessary. In this regard, feedback from PDs[3] is an important source of information for identifying market preferences and sentiment. A more detailed discussion of measures to support market liquidity is provided in Section 3.6.

Sovereign debt managers actively participate in debates on the microstructure of financial markets, including regulatory changes and trade execution mechanisms, as a way to improve functioning of markets. Their role in promoting secondary market liquidity of government bonds has become more prominent in light of structural and temporary changes to the market in the aftermath of the GFC (Global Financial Crisis). For example, they manifested their concerns over financial sector adjustments to the new regulatory environment in financial markets, particularly the potential adverse impact on liquidity in secondary markets (OECD, 2011 and 2014).

As financial market structures evolve, DMOs develop new solutions to address new challenges in government securities markets. For example, during the GFC, some DMOs were involved in addressing the malfunctioning of some segments of the government securities markets (OECD, 2014). Responses to the 2017 OECD survey on "Liquidity in secondary government bond markets" indicate that weakening liquidity conditions in certain segments of the bond market remain a critical challenge in several jurisdictions. The following section provides a summary of DMOs observations and views on the changes to liquidity in their secondary government bond markets.

3.3 DMOs observations on market liquidity: Concerns eased but remain considerable

The new financial landscape that emerged in the aftermath of the GFC has had significant implications for liquidity in government securities markets. During the past decade, sovereign debt mangers in several jurisdictions have observed constantly changing market liquidity conditions, reflecting various factors including new financial regulations, unconventional monetary policies and development of new technologies which are elaborated in *Section 3.5*. In this regard, the OECD survey of liquidity in secondary government bond markets, which aims to capture sovereign debt mangers' views on: market liquidity conditions, the factors driving change and to identify DMOs actions to support market liquidity, has revealed important policy implications since 2013.

Sovereign debt managers emphasise that even when market liquidity is ample in 'normal' times, it can evaporate quickly during stress periods which can exacerbate significant price movements and reduce confidence in government bond markets. Therefore, they are cautious about judging the robustness of liquidity conditions in sovereign debt markets. For example, in the wake of the GFC, sovereign debt managers observed sudden shifts in investor sentiment and some faced high liquidity risks which raised severe obstacles in primary market operations, resulting in a loss of market access in some extreme cases. Similarly, during the May-June 2013 turmoil when investors reacted to the Fed's potential reduction in its bond buying programme, sovereign debt managers, particularly in emerging markets, faced a violent sell-off in government bond markets which manifested in widened bid-ask spreads and decreased market depth. That event, once again, highlighted the fragile nature of market liquidity. In response to liquidity pressures, rapidly rising borrowing requirements and strongly risk-averse investor behaviour during the GFC, several DMOs were initially forced to follow a flexible issuance policy and modified one or more (technical or operational) features of their issuance procedures to adapt rapidly to shifting market conditions. Most notably, many DMOs have become more flexible which in turn has led to less predictable issuance strategies (OECD, 2014).

In parallel to market normalisation in the aftermath of the GFC, while the imminent risk of market liquidity declined, the prevalence of other factors – more structural and thus more long-lasting – including the introduction of various post-crisis financial regulations and the development of new financial technologies, have led to massive changes in market structures (OECD, 2016). In the light of evolving market structures, several sovereign debt managers have articulated their concerns about the increased pressure on primary dealer systems due to stricter regulations, changing business and risk management practices and other potential risks stemming from high frequency trading, particularly algorithmic trading.

Survey results on observations of changes in liquidity conditions of domestic sovereign bonds

The 2017 survey results, which are provided in Appendix B, indicate enhanced liquidity conditions in some OECD countries, including Latvia, the Slovak Republic and Slovenia. Improvements in market infrastructures and in PD systems, as well as diversification of the investor base – particularly an increasing presence of real money investors – are listed as the main driving factors of better conditions in domestic market liquidity in these countries. Also, some respondents underlined that the inclusion of bonds in emerging market government bond benchmark indices helps to attract a larger pool of buyers and sellers, thereby enhancing secondary market liquidity of bonds. It is important to note that some countries, including Denmark, Turkey and, to some extent, the United Kingdom, reported relatively improved liquidity conditions following a set of policy measures taken by the respective DMOs to address fairly low market liquidity in recent years.

Around one-third of respondents (including Austria, Canada, Italy, Ireland, Sweden, Switzerland and Germany) continued to perceive deterioration in liquidity conditions in their local currency debt market – in terms of bid-ask spread, trading volumes, etc. – in recent years (Figure 3.1). Concern about impaired liquidity is more pronounced in countries where relevant central banks implement sovereign bond purchasing programmes, which imply scarcity effects associated with large central bank purchases described in Section 3.5.

Overall, compared to previous-year results, the share of sovereign debt managers observing "worse" market liquidity conditions has decreased considerably, while the share of respondents indicating "better" and "unchanged" conditions have increased proportionally (Figure 3.1). However, one should be cautious about interpreting the results, since some of the countries that previously reported deterioration in market liquidity have not seen any major changes. That said, market liquidity concern is still prevalent across major government securities markets, albeit to a lesser extent.

Figure 3.1. Observations of changes in liquidity conditions of domestic sovereign bonds in recent years: A comparison of responses between 2016 and 2017

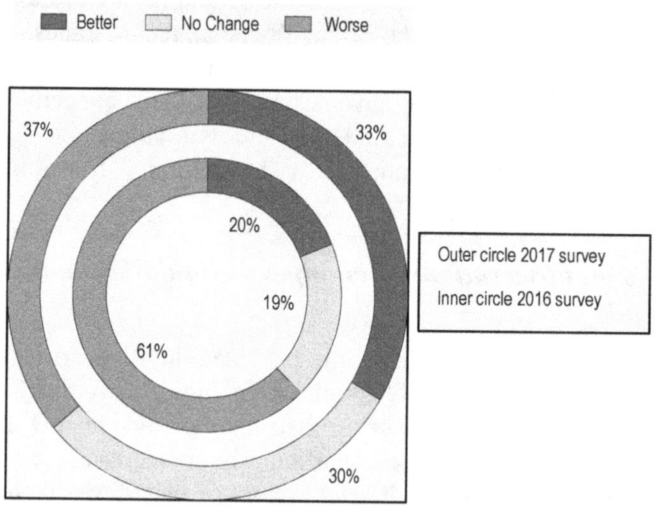

Source: OECD Survey on liquidity in secondary government bond markets (2016 and 2017).

StatLink http://dx.doi.org/10.1787/888933689748

As noted in the 2017 edition of the SBO, the US Treasury market remains one of the jurisdictions where secondary market liquidity has not been a major concern in recent years. It should be noted that developments, such as the rapidly growing share of exchange-traded funds (ETFs) and widespread use of electronic trading in the US Treasury market, have had important implications for secondary market liquidity of Treasuries, particularly of on-the-run securities (BIS, 2016).

Liquidity indicators for selected government bond markets

As discussed in Section 3.2, in order to assess market developments and capture different aspects of liquidity, such as depth, tightness and resiliency, DMOs closely monitor a number of liquidity indicators including bid-ask spreads and trade volumes. It should be noted that high frequency data (e.g. daily or intraday data) is critical to capture changes in liquidity and make a comprehensive liquidity assessment, while annual data provide insight into overall trends in secondary market liquidity structure. In this regard, Figure 3.2 and Figure 3.3 illustrate bid-ask spreads of 10-year benchmark bonds and trade volumes in Germany, Japan, the United Kingdom and the United States between 2006 and 2017. The annual spread levels on 10-year bonds which are usually regarded as one of the most liquid segments of the governments' yield curve surged during the GFC and European sovereign debt crisis, but have been quite stable at low levels in recent years. The year-to-year comparison of trade volumes presents a less clear picture in terms of market liquidity. In general, the annual changes in trade volumes decreased while financial markets have become less volatile in recent years. In Japan, although the scale of Japanese Government Bonds (JGBs) transactions is still a considerable amount, trade volumes of JGBs, excluding bond transactions with repurchase agreements, have shrunk more than 10% in 2015 and 20% in 2016.

Figure 3.2. **Bid-ask spreads of 10 year benchmark bonds in selected OECD countries, 2006 to 2017**

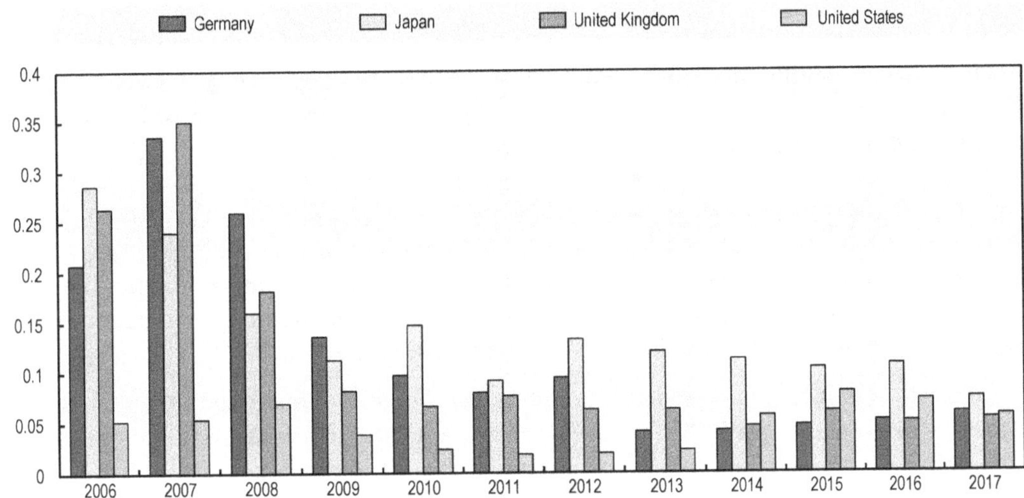

Notes: Bid-ask spreads are based on an average of daily close prices.
Source: Thomson Reuters and OECD calculations.

StatLink ⎯ http://dx.doi.org/10.1787/888933689767

Figure 3.3. **Trade volume changes in selected OECD countries, 2006 to 2016**

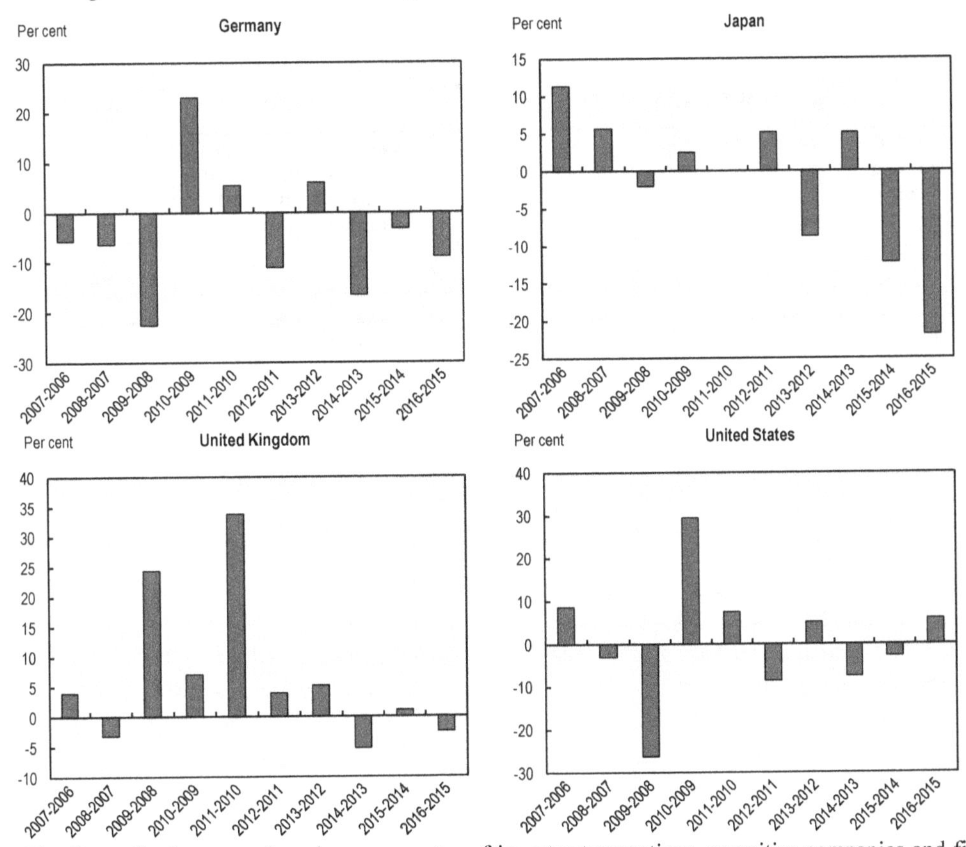

Notes: The figure for Japan are based on aggregates of investor transactions, securities companies and financial institutions excludes bond transactions with repurchase agreements; for the United Kingdom, Gilt-edged Market Makers (GEMMs) aggregate turnover data; for the United States, the Securities Industry and Financial Markets Association (SIFMA)'s trading figures; for Germany, Bund Issues Auction Group's reports.
Source: National authorities' websites and OECD calculations.

StatLink ⎯ http://dx.doi.org/10.1787/888933689786

71

3.4 Recent developments affecting market liquidity for government securities

Since the GFC, the global fixed-income market landscape has been changing constantly and rapidly due to a number of factors (structural and temporary). The changes, which include post-crisis regulatory reforms, central banks' purchasing programmes and FinTech[4] developments, are of paramount importance for secondary market liquidity. Several studies have been undertaken in recent years to investigate the impact of various developments on market liquidity conditions (e.g. ESRB 2016, BIS 2016, BlackRock 2017 and Bundesbank 2017). Although it is extremely difficult – if not impossible – to measure the precise impact of each of these factors on market liquidity, there is strong concern among market observers that market liquidity has been affected significantly by the ongoing evolution of financial markets.

In order to gain a deeper insight into the recent liquidity dynamics in the government securities market, the 2017 OECD survey on market liquidity asks DMOs views on the main reasons affecting liquidity of the government securities market (see Table 3.1). In response, countries that reported relatively low liquidity conditions underlined the adverse impacts of the following two factors: i) unconventional monetary policies, especially bond purchasing programmes, and ii) post- crisis regulatory reforms (Basel III, Solvency II, CACs, MiFID II, Dodd-Frank Act, etc.) The results in this respect are consistent with previous editions of the survey.

Table 3.1 **DMOs views on the main factors affecting liquidity**

	Number of answers[1]					
What are the main reasons affecting domestic liquidity conditions	Central bank policies	New regulations[2]	Investor base	Market infrastructure developments including rise in e-trading	Low interest rate environment	Credit ratings
2017 survey	13	11	9	6	5	5
2016 survey	13	14	7	3	9	6

1. In 2016 there were 23 responses, and in 2017 there were 28 responses. Countries could give more than one reason.

2. Regulatory changes in the financial system, including Basel III, Solvency II, CACs, MiFID II, Dodd-Frank Act, etc.

Source: OECD Survey on liquidity in secondary government bond markets (2016 and 2017).

Unconventional monetary policies, especially bond purchasing programmes

According to sovereign debt managers in the OECD area, the largest factor affecting liquidity in recent years is the impact of unconventional monetary policies. Following the GFC, large central banks implemented policy measures to deal with a challenging macroeconomic environment. With benchmark interest rates at, or close to, zero several central banks have adopted other monetary policy tools to provide additional monetary accommodation. In particular, the Federal Reserve, the European Central Bank (ECB), the Bank of Japan, the Bank of England (BoE), the Riksbank and the Swiss National Bank (SNB) have undertaken asset purchase programmes with the aim of lowering long-term yields. Furthermore, four central banks in Europe (i.e. the ECB, the Danish Central Bank, the Riksbank and the SNB) and the Bank of Japan have moved their policy rates into negative territory. As discussed in detail in previous editions of the SBO, low interest rates and asset buying programmes by central banks have affected, either directly or indirectly, all fixed income markets across the OECD. By design, these programmes have led to lower government bond yields, but have also contributed to unusually low interest rates across financial markets. Already low, sovereign bond yields have turned negative in some countries with over USD 9 trillion global sovereign bonds trading at negative rates at the end of August 2017, despite an upward trend in US rates and recent statements by monetary authorities in Europe.

As a direct result of quantitative easing programmes in recent years, central banks in Japan, the United States and the euro area have become major investors in local government debt securities (Figure 3.2). In Sweden, of the outstanding stock of central government marketable debt in Swedish krona, the Riksbank holds approximately 40% of outstanding stock of nominal bonds and 20% of inflation-indexed bonds (The Riksbank, 2017). In Japan, more than 40% of outstanding government bonds are held by the Bank of Japan. This means that a relatively large proportion of government bonds are not available for trade on the market, which could influence functioning of bond markets.

Figure 3.4 Central banks' holdings of domestic government debt, 2017

As a percentage of government debt

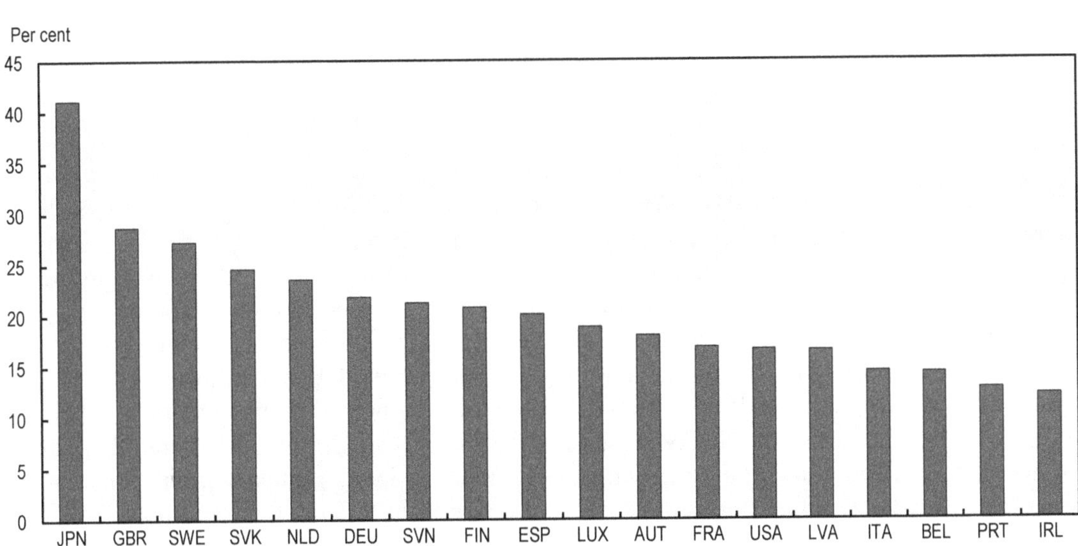

Notes: For all Euro area countries, estimates are based upon ECB holdings at market values as a proportion of general government debt at face values (Maastricht definition). All holdings are as of end December 2017, with the exception of Sweden which is as of end September 2017. Values have been aggregated by using fixed exchange rates, as of 1st December 2009.

Source: 2017 Survey on Central Government Marketable Debt and Borrowing carried out by the OECD Working Party on Debt Management; OECD Economic Outlook No. 102, ECB, central banks of Japan, Sweden, the United Kingdom and the United States.

StatLink http://dx.doi.org/10.1787/888933689805

Figure 3.5 **Selected central banks' holdings of domestic government debt, 2017**

USD

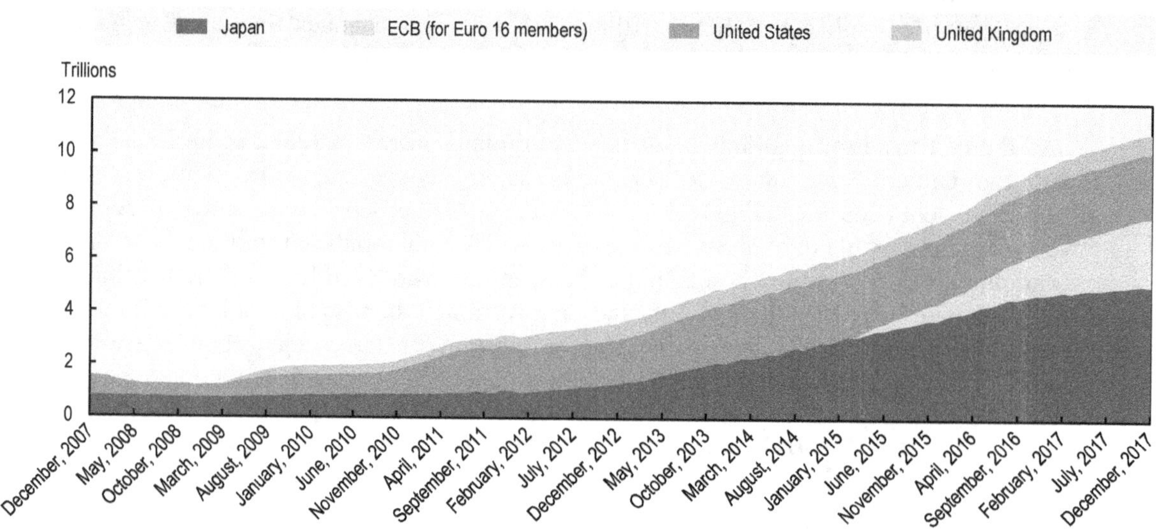

Notes: Values have been aggregated by using fixed exchange rates, as of 1st December 2009.

Source: ECB, central banks of Japan, United Kingdom and the United States.

StatLink http://dx.doi.org/10.1787/888933689824

As discussed in the 2017 SBO, the implications of central banks' actions for government securities market liquidity are not immediately clear. On the one hand, persistently low policy rates, coupled with asset purchasing operations, have supported bond valuations, reduced volatility and facilitated bond issuance in fixed income markets, although to different degrees across different market segments (e.g. sovereign bond cash versus repo markets) (BIS 2016). Also, it has been argued that central banks' large purchases of sovereign bonds have supported liquidity by providing a constant and stable source of demand in the market (Iwatsubo and Taishi, 2016). On the other hand, there are rising concerns about the unintended impact of unconventional monetary policies in some jurisdictions where central banks have become major investors in sovereign debt. One of the sources of this concern is that central banks buy and hold securities until they mature, hence they are not active traders by nature. This, in turn may have contributed to the perceived decline in market liquidity. Another reason is the scarcity impact associated with large purchasing programmes. In this respect, several DMOs have continued to highlight that increased holdings of domestic and foreign central banks might have had an adverse impact on liquidity. As central banks purchase sovereign bonds on a large scale from the markets, this has reduced the total stock of sovereign bonds available for trading. The relevance of scarcity effects of large-scale bond purchasing programmes in markets has been widely investigated in recent years (IMF, 2015). For example, drawing on intra-day transaction-level data for German government bonds purchased under the Public Sector Purchase Program (PSPP) of the ECB, Schlepper, Kathi, *et. al* (2017) find that the induced scarcity by asset purchase policies has an adverse impact on liquidity conditions, as measured by bid-ask spreads and inter-dealer order book depth. Specifically, their investigation reveals that the fall in liquidity is more evident in purchased, relative to non-purchased, German Bunds.

To address this scarcity concern and other potential issues (such as distorting relative prices), central banks have established or expanded their securities lending facilities, and attempt to act as "market neutral" as possible when purchasing securities. In this respect, the ECB adjusted the issue limit for purchases of specific bonds and issuer limit in 2015, and widened the list of PSPP eligible agencies in 2016. One of the important considerations given by central banks is the liquidity condition of different maturity segments to avoid disrupting orderly market functioning. For example, during quantitative easing programmes, the Fed aims to refrain from purchasing securities that are trading with heightened scarcity value in the repo market for specific collateral, or that are cheapest to deliver into active Treasury futures contracts.

While global liquidity conditions are still accommodative in several jurisdictions, the monetary policy stance has continued to diverge among the main OECD areas. After nearly a decade, the Fed began increasing its key policy rate in November 2016, while the policy stance has been broadly unchanged in the euro area and Japan. Also, the Fed announced in July 2017 that it will begin implementing its balance sheet normalisation programme in October. It is important to note that Treasury bonds account for 60% of the $4.2 trillion System Open Market (SOMA) portfolio, as of September 2017. Being transparent in its policy, the Fed described the unwinding process so that, instead of rolling over maturing Treasury securities in the SOMA portfolio, it will allow a fixed amount of those securities to mature without reinvestment, while the timing and size of adjustments will be subject to economic activities. Starting from October 2017, the Fed began gradually reducing its asset holdings by rolling off USD 6 billion of its Treasury securities holdings and USD 4 billion of agency debt and agency mortgage-backed securities maturing each month. In addition to potential broader market implications, the normalisation process will have an impact on the Treasury's issuance due to a funding gap created by less investment by the Fed.

While the Fed began increasing its key policy rate in December 2016 and unwinding its balance sheet in October 2017, the ECB and the BOJ continue with negative policy rates and asset-purchase programmes. The ECB noted that it will be continuing its net asset purchases, at least until the end of September 2018 or beyond if necessary, and in any case until the ECB sees a sustained adjustment in the path of inflation consistent with its price stability objective. In Europe and Japan, a large share of government bonds has been trading at record low levels, if not at negative yields (Chapter 1). Against this backdrop of abnormal asset pricing, there is great uncertainty about the behavior of investors in the case of monetary normalization, where interest rates are set on an upward path going ahead. Therefore, during the normalisation of monetary policies process in the United States and elsewhere, good communication and attention to liquidity developments across markets will be essential to avoid disruption (e.g. "taper tantrum" in the markets in 2013) to market liquidity in both advanced and emerging market economies.

Post-crisis regulatory reforms and recent efforts for calibration

The OECD liquidity survey results suggest the significance of post-crisis regulatory reforms (Basel III, Solvency II, CACs, MiFID II, Dodd-Frank Act, etc) for secondary government bond markets. Since the GFC, financial institutions, particularly banks, have faced increased regulations as regulatory authorities have sought to strengthen the resiliency of the financial system and reduce systemic risk.

As market makers, banks act as both agency traders to match buyers and sellers, and as principal traders stepping in to buy and sell securities on behalf of clients using their own balance sheets. Hence, primary dealer banks are seen as reliable liquidity providers as market-makers. As discussed in previous editions of SBO, Basel III standards and associated national regulation have broadly raised the cost of market-making activities. As a result, various regulatory initiatives have generally tried to reduce the risks that banks take on their balance sheet and the percentage of bank balance sheets available to support market-making activities. Sovereign debt managers highlight that the declining involvement of banks as "principal traders" due to regulatory reforms is an important factor affecting liquidity. It was reported that Austria, Denmark, Germany, Italy and the United Kingdom experienced an overall reduction in the amount of principal-based market making activities.

In response to the new financial market regulations which require more capital and impose restrictions on banks leverage, the WPDM has repeatedly stressed that regulatory changes in the financial system should strike the right balance between reducing risks – hence improving financial stability – and limiting the market-making abilities of banks (OECD 2011, 2014). Recently, there has been a growing effort in the United States to reduce the regulatory compliance burden and complexities in financial system without increasing the risk of another financial crisis. The US Treasury issued a number of reports which include a comprehensive set of recommendations to calibrate financial regulatory structure. The report titled 'A Financial System That Creates Economic Opportunities - Banks and Credit Unions' identifies that the cumulative effect of a number of bank regulations implemented in the post-crisis period may be limiting market liquidity. It recommends specific adjustments to regulatory requirements to address the unfavourable impacts these may have on market liquidity, including Supplementary Leverage Ratio (SLR) and enhanced Supplementary Leverage Ratio (eSLR),[5] as well as the Volcker Rule's limitations on proprietary trading[6] (The US Treasury Report, 2017). Similarly, in light of increasing concern about the adverse effects of the EU short-selling restrictions,[7] the European Securities and Markets Authority (ESMA) issued a consultation paper on the evaluation of certain aspects of this regulation in July 2017.

New regulations also require more regulatory reporting, greater transparency and disclosure, which ultimately increases operational costs in the financial services industry. For example, in Canada, the Client Relationship Model - Phase 2 (CRM2), which came into effect in 2016, asks financial institutions to produce two additional annual reports on costs and performance of their investments to disclose to their clients. In Europe, MiFID Level II, a major piece of post-crisis legislation which comes into effect as of January 2018, aims to strengthen protection for investors and bring greater transparency to financial markets by introducing additional, and somewhat more complex, reporting obligations to increase provisions for pre- and post-trade transparency (e.g. keeping online information up-to-date, providing future performance scenarios to clients for different market conditions, and requiring fund managers to pay directly for analyst research, instead of including it with other costs, such as trading commission). One recent initiative on increasing the quality and scope of post-trade data reporting has come from the United States; the recent 'Capital Markets Report' by the US Treasury underlines the need for regulatory changes to improve post-trade data reporting and collecting futures data.

Digital transformation in financial markets

Globally, the fixed income ecosystem is adapting to changing market dynamics and digital transformation is an important part of this process. In recent years, advances in technology have had an impact on market structures, by changing registration, clearing, settlement, payments, reporting and monitoring operations, as well as investment management services in financial markets (OECD, 2017). Developments, such as electronic trading venues and automated trading strategies, have enhanced transactional efficiency in financial markets. Applications of distributed ledger technologies (blockchain)[8] in finance, currently at an embryonic stage, have a strong potential to transform financial markets, especially fund transfers, bond issuance and trade settlement. While digitalisation in finance generates new prospects, including quicker, safer and cheaper financial transactions, it also brings new challenges such as cyber-risks, coding errors and other operational risks. Hence, this new digital trading landscape has multiple implications for fixed-income market liquidity.

One of the most significant developments is the growing use and variety of electronic trading platforms, such as Direct Streams, BrokerTec, Tradeweb and Liquidity Direct. These venues provide a continuous two-way market, via the web or special software, and enable investors to make ultra-fast executions at lower cost by directly matching buyers and sellers of bonds. This augments trading activities, which in turn enhances bond market liquidity. In several OECD jurisdictions (e.g. Italy, the United Kingdom and the United States), a considerable amount of trades – especially for on-the-run securities – are made through electronic venues. With regard to off-the-run securities, a recent example is Opendoor which offers free access to an all-to-all, session-based trading platform with a special focus on off-the-run US Treasury bonds. Such alternative venues may contribute to filling the gap left by traditional market makers and to liquidity in off-the-run securities. Alternative venues may also change the business model of primary dealers in the future as they see less investor flow.

While electronic trading platforms have lowered transaction costs and delivered significant efficiencies for market participants, execution models have created a number of undesirable side effects related to treatment of information and higher exposure to hacks and data breaches which may have an adverse impact on liquidity. Also, since such trading venues rely on complex digital systems, the possibility of an IT disruption to critical infrastructure rises, to causing significant market volatility, depending on their market share.

In addition to electronic trading platforms, high-frequency trading (HFT), algo-trading and robo-advice are other fast-growing applications of FinTech as a response to cost related challenges in asset management.[9] Automated trading systems are capable of (re)placing large amounts of trading among different markets in a fraction of a second, based on previously programmed trading strategies. In the United States, it is estimated that automated trading strategies account for more than half of trading activity in on-the-run treasury securities (TPMG, 2015). In general, automated trading systems have improved order entry speed at a lower cost and helped market makers to maintain tight yield spreads and consistent prices for closely related assets, which in turn supports market liquidity. However, it should be noted that the algorithms used (e.g. encoded trading strategies based on various technical indicators) in these systems may be similar across firms, meaning that market participation is less heterogeneous in behavior, leading to greater volatility. Also, it is possible for an automated system to experience anomalies (i.e. algo malfunctions) that could result in a false or a duplicate order a materialization of which could potentially trigger greater fluctuations in financial markets. One example is the flash-crash in the US Treasury market in October 2014, where the role of computer-driven trading on historical intra-day changes in 10-year bond yields has been pointed to in the Treasury's assessment report (US Treasury joint staff report, 2015). This incident served as a wake-up call for the US Treasury to monitor HFT activities more closely and improve reporting rules to cover HFT firms.

In addition to robo-advisors, FinTech innovations have important implications for passive investment strategies in asset management, such as index investing and exchange-traded funds (ETFs)[10] by increasing the range of investments that can be tracked by an index and enabling automatic trades. Specifically, ETFs that provide passive investment options with low management fees have been attracting investors over the past decade. There is a strong perception that ETFs act as a price discovery tool and increase market liquidity by providing intra-day purchasing and selling options to investors (BlackRock, 2016). Thus, pension funds and insurance companies are also investing in ETFs to maintain yield while improving liquidity in anticipation of market fluctuations (Central Bank of Ireland, 2017). However, this development raises questions about their transparency policy and to what extent ETFs are reliable liquidity providers in the bond market. In response, financial industry regulators in several jurisdictions have recently called for greater scrutiny of how the ETF industry works. In 2016, the US Security Exchange Commission introduced a new liquidity-management rule for Mutual funds and ETFs to ensure that funds can meet a surge of investor withdrawals. This measure also forces them to classify how long it would take to sell their holdings and requires disclosure of some metrics to shareholders.

Some market participants also note that ETFs in the bond market may not perform well under stressed market conditions, which may be contributing to a global 'liquidity illusion', disguising the true state of ability to trade positions on the bond market. Against this backdrop, sovereign debt managers acknowledge that there is a trend towards greater market-based intermediation through asset management entities, such as ETFs in government securities markets, while increased balance sheet costs have encouraged banks to shrink their market making activities following the post-crisis regulatory reforms. However, they emphasise that, unlike other participants in securities markets, PDs are reliable liquidity providers as market-makers since they execute trade orders from clients, even during the short-term supply and demand imbalances in the market, as they commit their own balance sheets.

More recently, growing applications of distributed ledger technology (DLT), or blockchain technology, in finance have great potential to transform financial market microstructures. Central bankers and stock exchanges of many countries (e.g. Australia, Singapore and the United States), are looking at ways of applying distributed ledger technology (DLT) or blockchain technology to trading, clearing and settlement systems. For example, in December 2017, the Australian Securities Exchange (ASX) became the first major bourse to announce the adoption of blockchain technology to record shareholdings and manage the clearing and settlement of equity transactions. Also, a few companies have issued bonds via blockchain during the last year. A wider adoption of this technology has the potential to result in i) cost reduction for back-office operations, ii) shortening of settlement time and iii) large gains in transparency, all of which allow greater efficiency in financial markets. However, given its early development stage, it would be premature to make a concrete assessment of its impact on bond market liquidity.

Lastly, one area where market participants have streamlined their operations through use of new technologies is associated with regulatory compliances. Financial services firms have been seeking ways to lessen costs of implementation and monitoring of new requirements of financial regulations in recent years. This environment has naturally reinforced technology-based solutions for regulatory reporting – also called RegTech. In this respect, software programmes and other digital solutions, create not only cost savings and efficiencies, but also improve functionality and reduce regulatory risk.

Increasingly digitalisation in finance has strengthened and quickened connections between different segments of financial markets, which can lead to idiosyncratic shocks (e.g. a malfunctioning of algorithms) being transmitted to other markets very quickly. This underpins the concern expressed by sovereign debt managers about correlated trades in the government securities market. Therefore, sovereign debt managers stress the significance of i) an evolving supervisory framework to keep pace with the new market structure by the regulatory authorities to ensure transparency in capital markets, and ii) employing a strong internal risk control environment by market participants to deal with the risks associated with automated trading, including operational risk (e.g. impairment of the electrical grid and algo malfunctions), cyber-security risk and counterparty risk.

This section briefly discussed how various market dynamic forces have altered the fixed income landscape and how these changes have affected the secondary market liquidity of government securities in recent years. Furthermore, demand for innovative investment products and services will continue, spurring further market structure innovation in the future, given that individual investors' behaviour will continue to change with the rise of the "millennials",[11] the largest and most technologically adept generation in history, This, in turn, ensures that the broad trend towards electronic trading, and other FinTech innovations, in fixed income markets will continue.

3.5 DMOs' experience with policy tools in addressing liquidity concerns

An efficient financial market promotes liquidity which, in turn, helps all market participants to find buyers and sellers more effectively. While greatly benefiting from operationally and informationally efficient markets, DMOs often play an important role in developing and securing well-functioning markets. Sovereign debt managers, as major borrowers, identify sources of stress, participate in debates, take action and implement policies in order to promote market liquidity.

In cases of exacerbated liquidity conditions, DMOs take proactive and sometimes innovative steps to address potential risks associated with deteriorating market liquidity. Worsening liquidity conditions may turn into a vicious circle, as lower liquidity in a certain segment of the market could make trade in that market less attractive. Contrarily, when there is a positive development in liquidity, such as when securities are included in certain indices due to their size or credit quality, these securities become more attractive for a larger pool of buyers and sellers, which in turn enhances liquidity further.

Sovereign debt managers have a wide range of proven tools at their disposal to enhance the degree of liquidity in the government securities market, including the benchmark bond programme, security lending facility and the PD system. A descriptive summary of these liquidity enhancement policy tools is presented in Box 3.1 under two categories, namely primary market operations (i.e. issuance procedures and policies) and secondary market operations. OECD's survey of liquidity in secondary government bond markets indicates that DMOs use some of these tools on a regular basis as integral parts of their debt management programme in order to support market liquidity. In addition to the policy tools described in Box 3.1, sovereign debt managers also react to such liquidity concerns (particularly those which stem from increasing investors concentration) by intensifying their efforts to achieve a more balanced mix of investors, and focus on bringing in new investors with diverse mandates and investment horizons.

Issuing a certain minimum quantity of bonds is considered vital to support secondary market liquidity as it enables more efficient price discovery and smooth functioning of markets. Therefore, building benchmark bonds at key maturity segments is one of the most common strategies among DMOs (Appendix B). While small issuers (e.g. Denmark, Finland and Sweden) concentrate on a limited number of benchmark bonds to avoid fragmentation, large issuers including Japan, the United Kingdom and the United States, have a number of bonds with benchmark status. Both large and small issuers (e.g. Austria, Germany, Japan, Latvia, Slovenia and Turkey) use tap-sales and/or re-opens to support existing lines of key benchmark bonds. Likewise, bond buyback operations "on a switch basis" and "on cash-basis" are often used to enhance volume of on-the-run issuance, at the expense of off-the-run bonds in the former case. In terms of bond buy-back operations, survey results indicate that some countries, including Belgium and Denmark, have regular programmes while others (e.g. Austria, Canada, France, Italy and Spain) adopt a discretionary approach.

One country's notable example in this area is Japan's "Liquidity Enhancement Auctions" (LEA), in practice since 2006: This special auction programme is designed to maintain and enhance liquidity in the Japanese Government Bonds (JGBs) market by additionally issuing off-the-run bonds. The LEA programme initially focused on the long end of the yield curve. In light of the recent market demand for additional liquidity for shorter maturities, the issuance amount of LEAs has been increased while JGBs maturing in more than 1-5 years were included in the programme in 2016.

Country examples also suggest that Separate Trading of Registered Interest and Principal of Securities (STRIP) programmes have been very successful in enhancing market liquidity. First introduced by the US Treasury in 1985, STRIPs are now a part of government bonds markets in several countries including France, Germany, Japan, Korea and the United Kingdom.

One of the most common secondary market activities undertaken by the surveyed sovereign debt market agencies is securities lending facility (SLF). Securities lending can make significant contributions to bond market development as it promotes secondary market liquidity by helping market participants continuously quote prices and avoid delivery fails. Specifically, SLF can be useful for PDs who must comply with quoting obligations and often engage in short positions as part of their daily market-making activity. Some DMOs, including those of Australia, Canada, Germany, Israel and Sweden, act as a lender of last resort and offer repo facilities to PDs in order to reduce the risk of shortages and, in turn, enhance liquidity in government debt markets. Particularly, it has been proven to be a valuable tool during episodes of market stress. For example, the countries hit hardest by the GFC (e.g. Ireland and Spain) have provided repos and switches for PDs when required to assist with liquidity. Faced with reduced borrowing in government bonds and mounting concerns over liquidity conditions, the Swedish DMO has increased its repo facility significantly since the start of its Quantitative Easing Programme in 2015.

With regard to liquidity enhancement policy tools used in secondary market operations, the German Finance Agency is a noteworthy example. The agency retains a portion of the announced issuance volume in every auction and uses these securities in its secondary market activities on e-trading platforms and in the OTC market. While the volume of securities reserved for secondary market operations varies from auction to auction, historically the average amount is about 20% of the issuance volume.[12] The agency stresses that its secondary market activities: i) help spread the timing of financing activities, ii) support smooth trading in German government securities, and iii) provide daily and direct insight into the current supply and demand situation which contributes to structuring of the issuance calendar and auction allotment decisions.

In several OECD countries, besides their role in primary markets, PDs are important for their market knowledge, secondary trading role and significant investor connections. PD systems, in terms of privileges and obligations, can be designed to support market liquidity. For example, in several countries (e.g. Hungary, Ireland, the Netherlands, and Turkey) PDs have an obligation to quote two-way prices on the secondary market. Also, ranking PDs according to their secondary market performance is a common practice (e.g. Austria, Belgium, Italy and France). Based on their secondary market performance, primary dealers can be entitled to certain benefits such as access to non-competitive biddings, switch/buy-back operations and securities lending facility. The most recent country initiatives to enhance market liquidity are associated with modifications in obligations and privileges of PD systems (Appendix B). Specifically, some DMOs adjusted obligations of PDs in 2016. For example, the Turkish Treasury reduced the maximum spread between bid and offer rates of benchmark securities-quotes by PDs. Similarly, the Ministry of Finance of Israel introduced more demanding obligations in both primary and secondary markets including defining different maximum spreads based on bonds duration. The Finnish DMO has introduced a maturity weighting in ranking the PDs' secondary market trades.

In early 2017, the Danish DMO introduced a new PD model with the aim of enhancing liquidity in the market for Danish government bonds and hence lowering funding costs for the government (Danmarks Nationalbank, 2017a). According to the new model, the government offers an annual payment to the primary dealers based on their performance in secondary market trading.[13] The Danish DMO assessed the results in a report in December 2017. Analysis indicates that the new model has proven to be efficient for *i)* tightening bid-ask spreads *ii)* increasing turnover rates and *iii)* strengthening competition among PDs (Danmarks Nationalbank, 2017b). Similar compensation methods for PDs exist in a few small issuer countries, including Iceland and Sweden.

As discussed in detail in the previous section, the GFC has changed the issuance environment that debt managers operate in. This new environment is characterised by ongoing extraordinary monetary policy operations in several jurisdictions; changing financial institution behaviours in response to increased regulation; and the impact of new, more complex electronic trading systems and strategies on liquidity in government bond markets. In the light of these developments, debt managers often participate in debates and collaborative efforts with other stakeholders in financial markets (including regulatory authorities, primary dealers and trading platforms) to identify inefficiencies, as well as to create new solutions to address emerging challenges faced in government securities markets.

Box 3.2. **DMOs operational toolbox to support market liquidity**

Liquidity enhancement policy tools used in primary market operations

- *Benchmark bond programmes:* A benchmark bond is defined as a liquid security against which other securities are priced. Typically, DMOs build up benchmarks by issuing large volumes at key tenors (i.e. 3-, 5-, 10-, and 30-year maturity segments) across the yield curve. By providing an adequate supply of standardised securities, benchmark bond programmes help to enhance liquidity and thereby lower liquidity premia, or sometimes create negative liquidity premia.

- *Reopening auctions:* The purpose of a reopening is to issue additional amounts of a previously issued bond via an auction. Hence, re-openings have a different price and issue date than the initial issue of the security. It is the most common practice among OECD DMOs to address illiquidity in the secondary market. DMOs use reopening auctions in order to build larger supply in existing lines (i.e. benchmark bonds or other securities) in markets and to limit fragmentation which impedes market liquidity.

- *Tap sales:* Tap sales, where bonds are issued at their original face value, maturity and coupon rate, provide flexibility to debt managers. This selling technique enables DMOs to increase volume of and to meet market demand for existing lines of bonds without running an auction.

- *Frequency and size of auctions:* Auctions need to be at a certain size to attract investors. For a given borrowing amount, relatively large and less frequent auctions yield operational cost savings for DMOs, while frequent and smaller sized auctions may attract more bidders. For large issuers, adopting frequent and smaller-sized auctions in sovereign borrowing programmes can promote market liquidity of government bonds. However, smaller issuers may find it difficult to attract the attention of investors if auctions are too frequent. In this regard, small issuers try to maintain a sensible mix of syndications and auctions to secure motivation of the banks.

- *Primary dealer models:* Obligations and privileges of PD systems can be designed to improve market liquidity of government securities. In terms of market making, PDs are often obliged to provide continuous and effective two-way prices to their customers in government securities markets. Also, stricter rules (such as a rise in minimum bid amounts and narrower bid/offer spreads) for PDs can be introduced to enhance market liquidity. Besides obligations, privileges to PDs can also be adapted so as to encourage secondary market trades. For instance, PDs can be ranked – or even be compensated - according to their market making performance.

Liquidity enhancement policy tools used in secondary market operations

- *Bond buyback operations "on a switch basis" and "on cash-basis":* Typically, the most recently issued (on-the-run) bonds are more actively traded than older (off-the run) bonds at any point in time. Through buyback operations in exchange of cash or on switch basis, DMOs are able to strategically increase the size of on-the-run bonds at the expense of off-the-run bonds and extend the average life of outstanding debt profile. This instrument, which allows redemption of large benchmark bonds before their maturity, is also effective in smoothing out debt redemption profiles, in turn, managing refinancing risk and liquidity risk. However, sovereign debt managers are often cautious about using this facility, as buy backs of illiquid lines may crystalize illiquidity costs on the public sector's balance sheet.

> • ***Separate Trading of Registered Interest and Principal of Securities (STRIP) Programmes:*** Separating bond principal payments from interest payments creates an alternative form of bond which appeals to investors who prefer a single future payment rather than a stream of coupon payments. Hence, some DMOs allow investors to split a bond into zero-coupon securities (striping) to meet investor expectations, thereby broadening the investor base and increasing trading activities.
>
> • ***Security lending facility and repos:*** This facility allows DMOs to act as a lender of last resort for primary dealers. This is a valuable tool to maintain balance between buyers and sellers in stressed market conditions, reduce the risk of shortages, avoid settlement problems and in turn enhance liquidity in government debt markets.
>
> • ***Secondary trading operations:*** In order to support market liquidity and to acquire market intelligence, a few DMOs operate in the secondary market or even have secondary trading functions. In the latter case, DMOs set up a separate trading room to buy and sell in the secondary government securities market within pre-defined limits.
>
> *Source:* Responses to 2017 OECD survey of liquidity in secondary government bond markets.

A notable measure taken recently by the US Treasure market to address market inefficiencies was the introduction of "fails charge trading practices". . Experiencing persistent and large settlement fails in the Treasury securities market during the GFC, market participants and authorities recognised that this situation can damage Treasury market liquidity – and have a negative impact on capital markets more generally – and worked together to improve market practices in the settlement process. In 2009, as a result of collaborative efforts, the Treasury Market Practices Group (TMPG)[14] introduced a new convention called "fails charge trading practices" for US Treasury and agency debt securities to incentivise timely settlement of security trade. The new convention promotes a penalty charge for the failing party in the case of a delivery failure (TMPG, 2016). This example of an innovative and timely response to market inefficiency cleaned up the large settlement fails in trade activities. Furthermore, in response to a relative rise in settlement fails, including the rise in fails for small-sized trades in 2016, the fails charge trading practice was modified and a minimum threshold[15] was applied for fails in markets. The recent revision aims to facilitate adoption of the fails charge practices and minimise the operational burden associated with it.

Notes

1. Government bonds are used for collateral in financial markets as they minimise credit and liquidity risks in transactions. They account for more than 80% of collateral used in repo markets in Europe and for about two-thirds of the repo market in the United States (ICMA, 2017).

2. Liquidity premium is a risk premium demanded by investors to compensate for uncertainty of the ability to sell a security easily for its fair market value.

3. Primary dealers (PDs) are financial institutions (i.e. banks or securities firms) that are entitled to buy government securities in primary markets with the intention of reselling them to others, thus acting as a market maker of government securities. The results of the 2016 survey among WPDM members indicate that 30 OECD countries have PD systems with various practices of obligations and privileges for members.

4. The term Fintech refers to a variety of innovative business models and emerging technologies that have the potential to transform the financial services industry https://www.iosco.org/library/pubdocs/pdf/IOSCOPD554.pdf

5. Recommendations include exceptions of the following items from the denominator of SLR and eSLR: (1) cash on deposit with central banks; (2) US Treasury securities; and (3) initial margin for centrally cleared derivatives (The US Treasury Report, 2017).

6. With regard to the Volcker Rule, recommendations that could have a significant impact on US Treasury markets include the following key points: i) banks with USD 10 billion or less in assets should not be subject to the Volcker Rule; ii) proprietary trading restrictions of the rule should not apply to banks with greater than USD 10 billion in assets unless they exceed a threshold amount of trading assets and liabilities; and iii) reduction of the complexity of the Volcker Rule to decrease regulatory compliance burdens; simplification of the definition of proprietary trading; allow banks to more easily hedge their risks and conduct market making activities (The US Treasury Report, 2017).

7. EU regulation on short selling and certain aspects of credit default swaps came into force on 1 November 2012. The main objective was to increase the transparency of short positions held by investors in certain EU securities and to reduce settlement risks and other risks linked with uncovered or naked short selling. https://www.esma.europa.eu/regulation/trading/short-selling

8. Distributed Ledger Technologies (DLT), or blockchain technologies – the same type of technology that underpins the bitcoin cryptocurrency.

9. Robo-advice refers to digital investment guidance and portfolio management services based on algorithms and computer programmes. The number of robo-advisor start-ups are increasing, particularly in the United Kingdom and the United States (e.g. IG, Santander and RBS).

10. Exchange Traded Funds (ETFs) offer intraday electronic trading of organised exchanges on broadly diversified baskets of bonds that typically track indexes. According to ETFGI, a research firm on trends in the global ETF ecosystem, the number of ETFs increased by five thousand while total net assets under ETFs management reached $4 trillion by the end of August 2017 (www.etfgi.com).

11. People born between 1980 and 2000 are called "Millennials"; they are regarded as the most technologically adept generation in history.

12. The overall amount held by the German Finance Agency is fixed by the Federal Budget Act at 10%volume of Federal bonds, Federal notes, Federal Treasury notes and Treasury discount papers in circulation (www.deutsche-finanzagentur.de/en/).

13. Payments of up to Krona 25 million are to be distributed among the central government's 11 primary dealers according to the following criteria: i) fulfilment of a number of minimum requirements for price quotation; ii) ranking according to price quotation; iii) customer turnover (Danmarks Nationalbank, 2017a).

14. The Treasury Market Practices Group (TMPG) is a group of market professionals committed to supporting the integrity and efficiency of the Treasury, agency debt and mortgage-backed securities markets in the United States. https://www.newyorkfed.org/tmpg

15.   The Treasury Market Practices Group (TMPG) recommends aggregation of fails charges between two counterparties for a given calendar month and introduced the application of a minimum threshold for fails. A claim is made if the aggregate charges for fails with a counterparty for a given calendar month exceed USD 500 (TPMG, 2016).

References

Bank for International Settlements, (2014) "Market-making and Proprietary Trading: Industry Trends, Drivers and Policy Implications", CGFS Papers No.52 www.bis.org/publ/cgfs52.pdf

Bank for International Settlements, (2016) "Fixed Income Market Liquidity", CGFS Papers No.55; www.bis.org/publ/cgfs55.pdf

Bao, Jack, Maureen O'Hara, and Alex Zhou (2016). "The Volcker Rule and Market-Making in Times of Stress", Finance and Economics Discussion Series 2016-102. Washington: Board of Governors of the Federal Reserve System; https://doi.org/10.17016/FEDS.2016.102.

BlackRock View Point (2017), *"A Primer on ETF Primary Trading and the Role of Authorized Participants"* March 2017; https://www.blackrock.com/corporate/en-at/literature/whitepaper/viewpoint-etf-primary-trading-role-of-authorized-participants-march-2017.pdf

Central Bank of Ireland (2017), "Exchange Traded Funds", Discussion Paper; https://www.centralbank.ie/docs/default-source/publications/discussion-papers/discussion-paper-6/discussion-paper-6---exchange-traded-funds.pdf?sfvrsn=6

Christensen, Jens H.E., and James M. Gillan (2016). "Does Quantitative Easing Affect Market Liquidity?" Federal Reserve Bank of San Francisco Working Paper 2013-26; *www.frbsf.org/economic-research/publications/working-papers/wp2013-26.pdf.*

Clark J. and Gabriel Mann (2016), "A Deeper Look at Liquidity Conditions in the Treasury Market" May 2016, The US Treasury Notes; https://www.treasury.gov/connect/blog/Pages/A-Deeper-Look-at-Liquidity-Conditions-in-the-Treasury-Market.aspx

Cimon, D and C Garriott (2017), "Banking Regulation and Market Making", Bank of Canada Staff Working paper 2017/7; www.bankofcanada.ca/wp-content/uploads/2017/02/swp2017-7.pdf

Danmarks Nationalbank (2017a), "Enhanced Requirements and Payments are to Strengthen the Danish Government Securities Market", Analysis No. 2, Copenhagen; www.nationalbanken.dk/en/publications/Pages/2017/01/Enhanced-Requirements-and-Payments-are-to-strengthen-the-Danish-Government-Securities-Market.aspx

Danmarks Nationalbank (2017b), "New Primary Dealer Model Continues in 2018", December 2017, No. 26, Copenhagen; www.nationalbanken.dk/en/publications/Documents/2017/12/Analysis%20-%20New%20primary%20dealer%20model%20continues%20in%202018.pdf

Das Udaibir S., M. Papapioannou, G. Pedras, F.Ahmed, and J. Surti (2010), "Managing Public Debt and Its Financial Stability Implications", IMF Working paper No: WP/10/280; https://www.imf.org/external/pubs/ft/wp/2010/wp10280.pdf

Deutsche Bank Research (2017), *"Robo-advice – a True Innovation in Asset Management"*, EU Monitor Global financial markets, August 2017;
https://www.dbresearch.com/PROD/RPS_EN-PROD/PROD0000000000449125/Robo-advice_-_a_true_innovation_in_asset_managemen.PDF

Duffie, D (2012), "Market Making under the Proposed Volcker Rule", Rock Center for Corporate Governance at Stanford University, Working Paper no. 106;
https://www.federalreserve.gov/SECRS/2012/January/20120118/R-1432/R-1432_011712_88664_334954090642_1.pdf

European Systemic Risk Board (2016), "Market Liquidity and Market-making", October 2016;
https://www.esrb.europa.eu/pub/pdf/reports/20161005_market_liquidity_market_making.en.pdf

Iwatsubo, K. and T. Taishi (2016), "Quantitative Easing and Liquidity in the JGB market", the Bank of Japan IMES Discussion Paper Series 2016-E-12, September 2016; https://www.imes.boj.or.jp/research/papers/english/16-E-12.pdf

Kurosaki, T., Y. Kumano, K. Okabe and T. Nagano (2015), *"Liquidity in JGB markets: an Evaluation from Transaction Data"*, Bank of Japan Working Paper no. 15-E-2
https://www.boj.or.jp/en/research/wps_rev/wps_2015/data/wp15e02.pdf

OECD (2011), "Regulatory Reform of OTC Derivatives and Its Implications for Sovereign Debt Management Practices: Report by the OECD Ad Hoc Expert Group on OTC Derivatives", OECD WP on Sovereign Borrowing and Public Debt Management, No. 1, OECD Publishing, Paris;
http://dx.doi.org/10.1787/5k9gz2n0sgq2-en

OECD (2014), *OECD Sovereign Borrowing Outlook 2014*, OECD Publishing, Paris;
http://dx.doi.org/10.1787/sov_b_outlk-2014-en

OECD (2016), *OECD Sovereign Borrowing Outlook 2016*, OECD Publishing, Paris;
http://dx.doi.org/10.1787/sov_b_outlk-2016-en

Schlepper, K., H. Hofer, R. Riordan, and A. Schrimpf (2017), "Scarcity Effects of QE: A transaction-level analysis in the Bund market", Discussion Paper No 06/2017, Deutsche Bundesbank, Frankfurt am Main.
https://www.bundesbank.de/Redaktion/EN/Downloads/Publications/Discussion_Paper_1/2017/2017_09_25_dkp_28.pdf?__blob=publicationFile

The RiksBank (2017), "The Riksbank's strategy for a gradual normalisation of monetary policy"', December 2017, Stockholm, Sweden;
https://www.riksbank.se/globalassets/media/rapporter/ppr/engelska/2017/171220/rap_ppr_171220_en_v19k33eyu.pdf

The US Department of Treasury (2015), "The U.S. Treasury Market on October 15, 2014", joint staff report of U.S. Department of the Treasury, Board of Governors of the Fed System, Federal Reserve Bank of New York, SEC and CFTC, July 2015, Washington DC, .; https://www.treasury.gov/press-center/press-releases/Documents/Joint_Staff_Report_Treasury_10-15-2015.pdf

The US Department of Treasury (2017), "A Financial System That Creates Economic Opportunities - Banks and Credit Unions", June 2017, Washington

DC.;https://www.treasury.gov/press-center/press-releases/Documents/A%20Financial%20System.pdf

The Securities and Exchange Commission (2016), "The Letter to FINRA about Regulation of U.S. Treasury Securities", August 2016, Washington DC https://www.sec.gov/divisions/marketreg/letter-to-finra-regulation-of-us-treasury-securities.pdf

The Treasury Market Practices Group (2016), "U.S. Treasury Securities Fails Charge Trading Practice", July 2016, New York; https://www.newyorkfed.org/medialibrary/microsites/tmpg/files/Fails-Charge-Trading-Practice-2016-07-13.pdf

ANNEX 3.A1

Methods and sources

Calculations, definitions and data sources

- The OECD area denotes the following 35 countries: Australia, Austria, Belgium, Canada, Chile, Czech Republic, Denmark, Estonia, Finland, France, Germany, Greece, Hungary, Iceland, Ireland, Israel, Italy, Japan, Korea, Latvia, Luxembourg, Mexico, Netherlands, New Zealand, Norway, Poland, Portugal, Slovak Republic, Slovenia, Spain, Sweden, Switzerland, Turkey, the United Kingdom and the United States.

- The OECD euro area includes 16 members: Austria, Belgium, Estonia, Finland, France, Germany, Greece, Ireland, Italy, Latvia, Luxembourg, Netherlands, Portugal, Slovak Republic, Slovenia and Spain.

- To facilitate comparisons with previous versions of the Outlook, figures are converted into US dollars using exchange rates from 1 December 2009, unless indicated otherwise. Where figures are converted into US dollars using flexible exchange rates, the main text refers explicitly to that approach. Source: Thomson Reuters. The effects of using alternative exchange rate assumptions (in particular, fixing the exchange rate versus using flexible exchange rates) are illustrated in Figures 1.3 and 1.4 of Chapter 1 of the *Sovereign Borrowing Outlook, 2016*.

- All figures refer to calendar years unless specified otherwise.

- For the bid-ask spread analysis, the OECD secretariat used Thomson Reuters data on 10 year benchmark bonds in selected countries. The daily bid-ask spread was calculated on each day using the bid close and ask close variables (where the ask price at least exceeded the bid price). For each calendar year an average of the eligible daily bid-ask spreads was calculated.

ANNEX A

OECD 2017 Survey on Primary Markets Developments

Annex A is available ONLINE ONLY at the following DOI:

http://dx.doi.org/10.1787/sov_b_outlk-2018-8-en

ANNEX B

OECD 2017 Survey on Liquidity
in Government Bond Secondary Markets

Annex B is available ONLINE ONLY at the following DOI:

http://dx.doi.org/10.1787/sov_b_outlk-2018-9-en

ORGANISATION FOR ECONOMIC CO-OPERATION AND DEVELOPMENT

The OECD is a unique forum where governments work together to address the economic, social and environmental challenges of globalisation. The OECD is also at the forefront of efforts to understand and to help governments respond to new developments and concerns, such as corporate governance, the information economy and the challenges of an ageing population. The Organisation provides a setting where governments can compare policy experiences, seek answers to common problems, identify good practice and work to co-ordinate domestic and international policies.

The OECD member countries are: Australia, Austria, Belgium, Canada, Chile, the Czech Republic, Denmark, Estonia, Finland, France, Germany, Greece, Hungary, Iceland, Ireland, Israel, Italy, Japan, Korea, Latvia, Luxembourg, Mexico, the Netherlands, New Zealand, Norway, Poland, Portugal, the Slovak Republic, Slovenia, Spain, Sweden, Switzerland, Turkey, the United Kingdom and the United States. The European Union takes part in the work of the OECD.

OECD Publishing disseminates widely the results of the Organisation's statistics gathering and research on economic, social and environmental issues, as well as the conventions, guidelines and standards agreed by its members.

OECD PUBLISHING, 2, rue André-Pascal, 75775 PARIS CEDEX 16
(20 2018 02 1 P) ISBN 978-92-64-29259-8 – 2018